Understanding
the Greek
Orthodox Church

Understanding the Greek Orthodox Church

Its Faith, History, and Practice

Demetrios J. Constantelos

The Seabury Press / New York

1982
The Seabury Press
815 Second Avenue
New York, N.Y. 10017
Copyright © 1982 by Demetrios J. Constantelos
Printed in the United States of America

Library of Congress Cataloging in Publication Data
Constantelos, Demetrios J.
    Understanding the Greek Orthodox church.

    Bibliography: p. 166.
    Includes indexes.
    I. Orthodox Eastern Church.   2. Orthodoxos
Ekklēsia tēs Hellados.   I. Title.
BX320.2.C66   281.9'3   81-21313
ISBN 0-8164-0515-8   AACR2
ISBN 0-8164-2367-9 pbk

For
my *kat'oikon ekklesian*
Stella,
Christine, John, Eleni, Maria
with
Saint Paul's admonition
"Stand firm and hold to the
traditions which you were taught
. . . either by word of mouth or by letter"
2 THESSALONIANS 2:15

"In him [God] we live and move and have our being; . . . For we are indeed his offspring"

Aratos
(Greek poet,
4th century B.C.)
as cited by Saint Paul, Acts 17:28

"In many and various ways God spoke of old to our fathers by the prophets; but in these last days he has spoken to us in the Son, whom he appointed the heir of all things, through whom also he created the world."

Hebrews 1:1–2

"Our Lord Jesus Christ, the Logos of God, of his boundless love, became what we are that he might make us what he himself is."

Saint Irenaios
(Greek Church Father and Bishop of Lyons,
2nd century A.D.)

The Refutation of False Gnosis
(Elenchos pseudonymou gnoseos)
v. praef.

Contents

Prologue

The present work is not intended for specialists but for the educated laity as well as for students of undergraduate liberal arts colleges and seminaries. I hope, however, that advanced students and other scholars will find here much of value. The approach to the subject is personal rather than academic.

Much of what is written here is a common heritage of all Orthodox Christians, but this book is concerned primarily with the Greek-speaking Orthodox, since there are several good manuals that deal with worldwide Orthodoxy. It seeks to explain their feelings and attitudes toward Christianity; to illuminate why the Greek Orthodox preserve a powerful historical consciousness and emphasize the importance of the Greek intellectual and cultural heritage in their religious experience. I hope the present work will serve as a stimulus to other Christians to further study Orthodoxy and as an invitation to the Orthodox of the other jurisdictions to provide monographs on their own churches and their own understanding of Christianity, which has never been monochromatic.

A few words of explanation: The emphasis on the Greek intellectual and cultural influence on Christianity should not be misunderstood as nationalistic or chauvinistic in nature. The simple fact is that the more I study history, the history of Greek antiquity in particular, the more convinced I become of the impact of ancient Greek language, thought, religion, and culture upon early and medieval Christianity. I am aware, of course, that this invites controversy and criticism. The problem is not new. The issue of Hellenism versus Christianity is as old as the Gospel of John, the letters of Paul, and the other writings of the New Testament. But it is common knowledge that before there was a Latin, an American, a Bulgarian, a Romanian, a Russian, or a Serbian Orthodox Christianity, there was a Christianity split into two parts: Jewish and Gentile, or Greek. Jewish Christianity disappeared, while Greek Christianity survived. Hence the emphasis on the Greek role in the history and thought of Christianity. There are many historical and intellectual reasons for emphasizing the influence of Hellenism on Christianity, as will become manifest in the analysis of several theological teachings. I examine Hellenism in two different sections: first as a *propaedeia* to, and second as an integral part of, early Christianity.

Because of the present volume's purpose, my approach has been multidisciplinary. I discuss anthropological, historical, and sociological aspects as well as doctrine, ethics, ecclesiastical history, apologetics, liturgy, and ritual. Perhaps in this approach lies both the strength and weakness of the book. Strength, because for the non-Orthodox reader a corpus of information has been gathered in the confines of a small volume. Weakness, because the book is exposed to criticism from specialists and experts of several disciplines.

Some of the materials here have previously appeared in *The Greek Orthodox Church* (New York, 1967), which is now out of print; *Marriage, Sexuality, Celibacy: A Greek Orthodox Perspective* (Minneapolis, 1975); and in the periodicals *Orthodox Observer, The Way* (England), *Journal of Ecumenical Studies, Concilium,* and *Jurist.* It appears here revised and in summary form. Some other materials have been delivered either as lectures or as sermons from the pulpit of St. Demetrios Church, Perth Amboy, N.J.; St. Nicholas Church, Lexington, Mass.; and St. Demetrios Church, Towson, Md.

I wish to thank my colleagues, Theodore Stylianopoulos, of Holy Cross Greek Theological School; Phocas Angelatos, formerly director of St. Basil's Academy and editor of the *Orthodox Observer;* and Joseph Walsh and Rachel Reeder, of Stockton State College, who read the manuscript, each from a different perspective, and offered me the benefit of their criticism.

Through this book, citations of Scripture, unless otherwise designated, are from the Revised Standard Version of the

Bible. Quotations are from the same source, except in a few cases where I have preferred my own translation.

It has not been found desirable to maintain absolute consistency in the transliteration of Greek names. Well-known names in English, such as Cyril and Constantine, appear in the usual English spelling. Otherwise the Greek spelling has been retained. The Latin form of a name, which may be more easily recognized by some readers, can frequently be determined by changing the *os* ending to *us*. Thus, Plotinos becomes Plotinus, and Irenaios becomes Irenaeus.

1

Religion as a Preparation for Christianity

Greek Orthodox Christianity derives its beliefs, doctrines, ethics, worship, and practice, from two sources, both of which use the term "revelation" to speak of hidden truth made apparent. One is known as natural, or "physical," revelation and the other as supernatural, or "metaphysical," revelation. While many religions speak of natural revelation, not all accept supernatural revelation as Christianity understands it; and while all religions share many elements that exist in natural revelation, Christianity's exclusiveness stems from its claims of supernatural truths revealed by specific agents and in particular by Christianity's own founder.

The term "religion" has been given many definitions. It derives from the Latin *religio,* which originally meant respect for what is sacred; later it came to mean holding fast to conscientiousness, to the instinct that is innate in the human being and that controls, prompts, approves, reprimands, and guides the human being in his or her relations with the surrounding cosmos and with fellow human beings. The Greek term for religion is *threskeia,* and *threskeia* means instinctive worship of the divine. According to some experts, *threskeia* derives from the verb *throsko,* which means to leap up in joyful expectation, to search. In this sense every human being instinctively behaves religiously, and in a way life itself is identified with religion, and religion is concerned with the whole of life.

The Divinity in History

How relevant is religion to modern man? Is he not a self-sufficient being who has dominated the world? As the ancient Greek dramatist Sophocles said in his *Antigone:* "Many are the wonders but there is no greater wonder than man." But man is a complex phenomenon, and religion is one of his many concerns. The manifestations of man's spiritual and intellectual life constitute what we call civilization.

The question, however, has been raised concerning the value of religion. It is not uncommon to find thoughtful, scientifically trained persons who regard religion as something outgrown, a parasite of civilization. Karl Marx announced that "religion is the opium of the people"; others have adopted the slogan "God is dead, and religion has been buried with him." Still others insist that they do not need religion ("I can be as good a person as any without it") or that religion is irrelevant to modern life.

These and other similar aphorisms could indicate, of course, a conscious or an unconscious anxiety about and concern with religion. For many people, God is very much alive, and to them religion appears just as vital in modern times as in centuries past.

Even without belief in God, one may be a good person and a fine citizen. But the advocates of religion in the Western tradition insist that there is no fullness of life without God.

Religion offers a combination of values indispensable—or at least very necessary—to life. Religion inspires the conviction that the great elements of our spiritual world are real and eternal and that there is no power, natural or human, that can obliterate them. Religion transfers the human spirit from the world of the profane to that of holiness and transcendence. It satisfies the natural human longing for infinity and for meaning.

Alexis de Tocqueville wrote: "Unbelief is an accident and faith is the only permanent state of mankind." Thus the study of religion rightly concerns modern people. Religion can make valid claims upon any human being, because it is not a blind force, demanding unquestioning acceptance, but a constant challenge to acceptable and widely held beliefs and opinions.

What people believe has much to do with the style of life they live and with the kind of influence they exert. To say that I believe only in the world of my senses, in what I see and experience, is to silence an inner voice that challenges the human to a perpetual quest. For as we are impelled to satisfy such needs as hunger and thirst, so we are impelled to satisfy an inner impulse that has been identified with religion. In fact, religion is the quest for the largest and the fullest satisfaction of man's loftiest needs. Man often commits fundamental injustices against himself because of ignorance or plain nonsense. He denies his spiritual nature by failing to take religion seriously.

Religion as a historical and psychological phenomenon is one of the many common elements in the life of humankind. Despite color or creed, people have common characteristics that indicate that they are of a common origin. The declaration that God has "made from one every nation of men to live on all the face of the earth . . . that they should seek God, in the hope that they might feel after him and find him" (Acts 17:26–27) may not satisfy a skeptic or an agnostic who does not believe in the authority of the Scriptures. But there are nonscriptural affirmations, to be found in the natural and psychological sciences.

Many modern scientists agree on the unity of the human race. Contemporary anthropologists, for example, who deal with the antiquity of man, the problems of race distribution, language, culture, and religion concur, despite disagreement over many other points, on two great subjects, namely the unity of the human race and the phenomenon of religious aspiration. Though the presumption of the psychic unity of mankind was much stronger among earlier students of comparative religion, it is not without strong advocates even today. There are other branches of knowledge that testify to this unity and solidarity of humankind. Anatomy and physiology reveal a physical unity in which there are not essential differences. Sociology and psychology confirm that the various races are, in a basic sense, intellectually and emotionally the same. The spiritual unity of humankind is proved by the existence of common or similar spiritual and religious experiences. It is also indicated by the essentially religious nature of the human being. Religious aspiration is common to most of mankind. Wilhelm Schmidt, an Austrian anthropologist and ethnnologist, writes: "Religion is one of the primary components of the human nature and is not to be connected with any such specific origins as magic, death, dreaming, mana or animism." To be sure, it embraces many emotions, such as fear, love, awe, and joy (but love is man's natural response to a religious object, as William James observes). However, religion is not a merely emotional response but a response that in one way or another is total, involving the whole person—intellect, emotion, and will.

Most human beings instinctively know what is right and what is wrong. Whether "civilized" or "primitive," every human being wrestles with questions pertaining to the origin and meaning of existence, the ultimate destiny and purpose of life— all questions religious in nature. Edmond de Pressensé writes that "religious sentiment is the peculiar characteristic of man; it is part of his very being. It is an intuitive and spontaneous development of his nature. He turns instinctively to the Divine as the magnet to the pole . . . . If man were not a religious being by nature, he would never become religious. Religion and spiritual thinking have their roots in the deepest aspirations of man." The biophysicist Lecomte du Nouÿ writes: "Independently of any rite, of any church, there has always existed in the world a religious spirit, a desire to believe, a desire to adore without restriction, a desire to humiliate oneself in total veneration, a desire to elevate oneself by approaching a conceivable but inaccessible ideal." Human nature is expected, not to share in hating (*synechthein*), but to share in loving (*symphilein*), in the words of Sophocles' *Antigone*. Arnold Toynbee says, "Religion itself . . . is an intrinsic faculty of human nature. I believe that being human involves having a religion and that human beings who declare that they have no religion are deceiving themselves through failing to research their own hearts."

The history of humankind reveals that two beliefs are practically universal: a belief in beings or a being superior to the human person and a conviction that existence is not limited to this world, but that there is continuity of life beyond the grave.

No people has ever attained a significant culture without religion. It has been one of the most powerful drives in the history of every race, nation, and civilization.

The religious spirit is hidden in the inner confines of our being, awaiting the event or the person capable of transforming it into full fruition, into faith and activity. Thus, according to Rudolf Otto, religion may be defined as the "response of the human being to the holy and righteous call of the eternal"; or "religion is the response of a person to the holy and righteous call of God."

Archaeologists and historians confirm that the religious beliefs of people have preoccupied the human mind since early antiquity. To paraphrase Homer, as young birds instinctively open their mouths for food, all men crave for gods. Plutarch, the ancient Greek biographer and historian, confirms the universality of religion when he writes: "You will find cities and towns without theaters, without public baths—cities even without walls but you will not find any cities without temples." Among those in antiquity who expressed affirmative views of religion are Socrates, Plato, Cicero, Plotinos. The philosopher Plotinos considered religion the elevation of the human being to God. Socrates and Plato thought of religion as the belief in divine providence. All of them spoke of its universality and of divine absolutes. Others, like Sophocles, emphasized the morality and the validity of the "unwritten laws," the superiority of divine commandments over human compulsion, divine absolutes over human compromises.

Not only has there been no recorded civilization without religion, but in fact, religion and civilization advanced together. In the words of A. Menzies: "Religion is the inner side of civilization and the study of it is the study of the very soul of its history." In all the great civilizations it has reflected persistently and vitally a great and central interest. In the history of the Egyptians, the Persians, the Chinese, the Indians, the Greeks, the Hebrews, and the Romans, religion has played a prominent role. In fact, history and anthropology, as well as other disciplines, confirm that in addition to technology (or the making of tools), language, and writing, religious beliefs and practices are major elements in distinguishing the human from other creatures. Anthropology has stressed not only the universality but also the continuity of all religious phenomena.

But religion has been many things to many people and societies. In ancient as well as in contemporary primitive societies, religion encompasses ethics, philosophy, theater, ritual, even science.

Cosmic Preparation

Religion is one of the most complicated phenomena in history. Some students of religion believe that the religious sentiment derives from a supernatural source: That as there is no creation without a creator, no religion without a god, so cosmic power is the source of religion and has been revealed in life during the course of many centuries in accordance with the maturity and development of humankind. Some believe that religion began in fear or wonder, as suggested by the Roman poet Lucretius and later by the philosophers Hobbes and Hume. Nevertheless it does not exist only in primitive cultures—a fact that refutes the frequently made claim that as soon as the primitive cultures disappear religion also disappears. And religion is expressed in a variety of ways, not simply in fear, but through "the feelings, the acts, the thoughts, and experiences of men," as the American psychologist William James observes. Others have attempted to explain the religious phenomenon as due to the fortuitous organization of various moral and esthetic elements, such as love and beauty, truth and honor, creative science, and human brotherhood. But religion is one expression in the whole realm of ethics, which, however, does not cover all aspects of religion. Salvation, for example, a very important element of religion, is something more than ethics and more essential than the mere moral betterment of man. Many religions teach that religion involves the defeat of death, the elimination of pain and sorrow, and an eternal life of joy.

According to the Christian Scriptures the human race received its religion by direct revelation from its creator—God. The human person as a limited creature was unable to find God by searching. Thus God revealed Himself.

On account of his divine nature, which he received at creation, the human person possesses a faculty for religion. What

the Bible testifies concerning the origin and nature of humankind is fully supported by the fact that the human being craves
the fellowship of a Supreme Being, a creator with whom it must
converse, for "In him we live and move and have our being
. . . for we are indeed his offspring," as the ancient Greek poet
Aratos put it and Paul repeated (Acts 17:28).

But what is religion? There is no exact and unchangeable
definition. The classical scholar Gilbert Murray writes that
"religion, like poetry and most other living things, cannot be
defined." In addition to the Greek and Latin definitions cited
earlier, there are several other definitions, such as that religion
is the recognition on the part of man of a controlling super-
human power entitled to obedience, reverence, and worship.
Another, possibly more satisfactory, definition is "the belief in
the existence of a Supreme Power, combined with a feeling of
dependence on Him, which permeates the whole personality,
brings it into a personal relation with Him and affects the whole
life of the individual and his relations with his fellowmen."
Seneca defined religion as the effort of man "to know God and
to imitate Him [*cognoscere deum et imitari*]."

Religion is one. Just as a tree has a single trunk, but many
branches and leaves, so there is one source and one religion,
which becomes many as it passes through the human medium.
There are five different recognizable expressions of religion,
namely mystical religious experience, religious feeling and ritual, ecclesiastical organization, intellectual doctrine, and ethics.
These aspects, which are often found together, can also be
found as separate functions. Ritual, for example, composed
virtually the entire religion of primitive people. But as man
advanced, ritual was linked with the ethical and doctrinal, and
so man's duty to God and to man likewise came to be regarded
as moral, doctrinal, and ceremonial. That is what happened in
the ancient Greek religion and even more pronouncedly in the
Hebrew religion.

The story of Old Testament religion is the story of a long
development. It began with the original knowledge imparted
to man at the time of his creation; it continued with the primitive religion of the earliest Hebrew nomads; and it culminated
in the ethical monotheism of the great Hebrew prophets.

Through Moses and the prophets, the worship of the one God was rediscovered, though monotheism did not prevail for many centuries. Old Testament religion went through stages of evolution emphasizing certain elements according to circumstances and needs. For example, at times religion required of the Hebrews only the limited obligations of fear, love, and service of God: "What does the Lord your God require of you, but to fear the Lord your God, to walk in all his ways, to love him, to serve the Lord your God with all your heart and with all your soul . . .?" (Deut. 10:12). Later Hebrew religion emphasized other aspects: "What does the Lord require of you but to do justice, and to love kindness, and to walk humbly with your God?" (Mic. 6:8).

There are students of religion, Christian theologians in particular, who, following Saint Paul's teachings, believe that non-Christian religions are corruptions of the earliest faith, the faith in the existence of one Supreme Being, the creator of heaven, of earth, and of humankind. It was this Supreme Being who presented himself originally to all mankind; who revealed himself to human thought, will, and feeling; manifested to all people, as his highest creatures, his being and acting, directly after the creation. Not only the Judeo-Christian witness, but comparative religion on the whole, conclude that the origin of religion is shrouded in the mystery of revelation.

The belief that religion has its origin in revelation presupposes the existence of two beings—the absolute being and the human being. Religion in its simplest form implies God and the human being. Their relationship is manifested through spiritual and moral activities. God commands and orders, while the human person obeys and executes God's commandments. Moreover, God reveals himself to the human race gradually, making known His energies and attributes, which determine its progress in its religious and human experience in accordance with various mental, hereditary, sociological, and even climatic factors.

For these reasons, religion has expressed the essential but changeable spirit of human life in various ages and nations. The religion of a people is in many ways an expression of its character, mentality, intellectual cultivation, and spiritual development. Every religion has principles of truth revealed by God either indirectly or directly, in accordance with the needs and characteristics of its followers. But these are not complete and self-sufficient religious truths.

What does religion stand for? What is its end? "Life, more life, a larger, richer, more satisfying and eternal life is the end of religion." Essentially religion is two-sided: It offers something and it demands something. From primitive times, religion has been conceived of as imparting spiritual goods. It offers an enhancement of courage, zeal, group unity, moral power, peace of soul and mind, and creative insight. But the inherent meaning of religion rests not in what it gives but in what it demands: belief, moral endeavor, worship, brotherhood, and spiritual aspiration.

Doctrine, ethics, and worship are interrelated and supply the bases of the religious life. All three are areas where religion makes demands upon life. Thus one cannot say that he need not be concerned with morality. Neither can one say that, if he possesses morality and belief in God, he need not worship.

The ultimate purpose of religion is the eternal salvation of the inner essence of the human being and the eternal preservation of the human spirit, which demands to be governed by ideal values. The human spirit is the most valuable entity in the universe, revealing the real nature of the creative power and the ultimate meaning of creation. It seems that the human spirit is the only eternal element in a world of change because it is part of the cosmic spirit, of God, and lives in God as an independent and autonomous unit.

While all religious creeds have made positive contributions to civilization, some represent fallacies and distortions of the human mind. For Christianity, that distortion led to the existence of a multitude of religious creeds and sects. The multiplicity of religions came into existence when the human being disavowed true knowledge of the creator.

The apostle Paul provides an account of how human beings failed to retain the true knowledge and revelation of God:

> What can be known about God is plain to them, because God has shown it to them. Ever since the creation of the world his invisible nature, namely, his eternal power and deity, has

been clearly perceived in the things that have been made. So
they are without excuse; for although they knew God they
did not honor him as God or give thanks to him, but they
became futile in their thinking and their senseless minds were
darkened. Claiming to be wise, they became fools, and ex-
changed the glory of the immortal God for images resembling
mortal man or birds or animals or reptiles (Rom. 1:19–23).

According, then, to the Christian viewpoint, the old faiths
retained but a partial revelation of the original truth: Hence,
all were imperfect and liable to error, and religion became
subject to a process of evolution and reinterpretation up to a
certain time. The widespread and deep-seated resemblances
between different religions and faiths—such elements as love
for one's enemy, prayer, regeneration, and expectation of judgment—are due, not necessarily to mutual limitation, but to
similar emotional reactions to the mystery of the world, the
needs of human nature, and primarily to the fact that religions
derive from the same source. In fact, the uniformities discern-
ible in religious beliefs, rites, and customs indicate the unity of
the religious consciousness of humankind.

It is conceivable that monotheism was the original form of
religion. Theologians who regard belief in one God as innate
in the human person are not alone. Many modern ethnologists
have abandoned the old belief in the emergence of monotheism
as part of a general intellectual and ethical evolution of the
race. Anthropologists too agree that monotheism was found
and is still being found among primitive races. Some nontheo-
logical scholars even suggest that an innate knowledge of revelation is the origin of the idea of God and of immortality, and
of the rites of prayer and sacrifice—that is, of religion in general. For example, the British anthropologist Paul Radin writes
that monotheism was developed by poets, philosophers, and
other primitive savants or individuals with a developed quality
of mind who observed the world as a unified whole. Radin
stressed the universality of monotheistic conceptions among
primitive wise men.

According to Wilhelm Schmidt, to whom we referred earlier,
the "High God" of all primitive peoples is eternal, omniscient,
beneficent, omnipotent, the creator of reality, the creator of

man. But belief in one God was distorted into animism, poly-theism, idolatry, cults of the dead, and other forms of religious beliefs, not only because of human sinfulness, but because of the fact that human societies became more complex. Dr. Schmidt concludes in his exhaustive work on the origin of the idea of God as follows:

> The idea of God came by revelation, and the evidence, massed together, analyzed and sifted with scholarly acumen, is altogether convincing. Thus we may say that at the begin-ning God, with the other gifts He gave to man, gave him religion. That is to say, He gave him not only a predisposition for reverence and piety, but also a certain amount of religious knowledge, such as that which He gave to the Hebrew people at the time of Moses and the Prophets.

Field studies made by more recent ethnologists give support to Schmidt's conception of an original monotheism in primitive religious experience. Nevertheless there are ethnographers who support other theories of the origin of religion, such as that it began in animism, totemism, or polytheism, or some combination of these. All these theories, however, remain con-jectural; there is no one definitive scientific account of the na-ture of primitive religious experience.

The principle, however, that *ex nihilo nihil fit* may be aptly applied in the sphere of religion: It must necessarily have a beginning, since nothing is produced from nothing, as the Latin axiom states. Independent of experience and knowledge, the human person has a preconceived tendency toward religion. This inclination springs from the innate idea of God that the person holds, as Descartes, who is the champion of this expla-nation, contends. That is, it belongs to the very nature of the human being to believe in and to worship God. Therefore, religion is not an arbitrary or artificial device or invention, as Marxists would have us believe.

The Hebraic Heritage

Greek Orthodox theology views ancient Hebrew religion as one of God's instruments propaedeutic (preparatory) to Christi-anity. To be sure, God, the Creator of the world, is not the exclusive possession or Lord of any one people, and there is no specific people that God favors or loves more than others. But it is neither unnatural nor illogical for the Creator to elect some persons—such as Noah, Abraham, Ikhnaton, Moses, Amos, Socrates, Plato, or others—and use them as special instruments in His historical purpose. In the language of the Old Testament a covenant between God and a tribal leader was a covenant between God and the tribe. Participation in the provisions of a covenant was never a matter of individual choice or a democratic procedure. Thus the sin of Adam became the sin of his descendants, the blessings on Abraham were blessings on his tribe, a curse on a leader was a curse on his followers.

According to the Genesis account, following the great flood which destroyed sinful mankind, the Creator made a covenant (Chapters 8 and 9) with Noah, the only survivor, who became a new genearch of mankind. The agreement between God and Noah provided that God would not allow another destructive flood, that He would remain the God of Noah's descendants, and that all mankind would be placed under divine promise and law. God guaranteed to preserve the natural order of things, and Noah's descendants, the ancestors of all nations, were to become subject to God's laws. But Noah's descendants walked after their own desires, and the result was a second alienation of the creation from the Creator.

Throughout history, and in various ways, God "did not leave himself without witness [*in Greek, amartyron*]" (Acts 14:17). However, at certain times He made new covenants for His purposes. Like Noah's, Abraham's covenant was of cosmic significance. According to the Genesis story (17:1-5), God said to Abraham: "I am God Almighty; walk before me, and be blameless. And I will make my covenant between me and you, and will multiply you exceedingly. . . . Behold, my covenant is with you, and you shall be the father of a multitude of nations." Two principles stand out in this covenant: that God is Almighty and that the "multitude of nations" that will come after Abraham should follow Abraham's example and walk blamelessly before God. The lordship of Abraham's God was reiterated in still another covenant, that between God and Moses, the universal significance of which lies in the issuing of the Ten Commandments. In both covenants, God appears in anthropomorphic terms and as an educator, a personal being in dialogue with man, a pedagogue directing and advising. The author of the Epistle to the Hebrews sums up the importance of all covenants between God and man before the Christian Era by emphasizing their preparatory nature. According to that author, Jesus Christ is not only superior to Abraham, Moses, and high priests of Old Testament times, such as Melchizedek, but he is also God's Son who brings to an end the stage of preparation and introduces the age of maturity, of freedom from the demands of the law (whose purpose was pedagogical), and of religious fulfillment.

The Old Testament is the story of God's gradual self-disclosure, gathering momentum as history moves on, from a narrow sphere and a slow movement to a far-reaching, cosmic, all-inclusive revelation. As Georges Florovsky has put it: "Ultimately, the Old Testament as a whole has to be considered as 'a book of the generation of Jesus Christ, the Son of David, the Son of Abraham' "(Mt. 1:1). It was the period of promises and expectation, the time of covenants and prophecies. To be sure, the Old Testament includes beautiful poetry and good legislation, but also much inhuman and ugly material that does not commend it as a religious or even as a humane book. In many passages in the Pentateuch and other books, the Israelites were ordered to exterminate the people of Canaan or other tribes in the belief that God had promised the land to the Hebrews (for example, see Deut. 7:1–10, 18–20; 9:4–5). The evidence is overwhelming that the ancient Hebrew religion was just as intolerant as Christianity would be in the Western Middle Ages. The spirit of the religious crusade originates in the Old Testament, where next to liberal legislation one finds descriptions of orgies of slaughter, and savage rules to justify the extermination of established tribes. But the Old Testament is rather the evolutionary process of God's disclosure, and the self-understanding of the national consciousness of a people. It is a manifestation of God's involvement in history exemplified in the life of various peoples, ancient Israel in particular. It tells both how God created and how He re-created mankind.

The central idea that brings together the literature of the Old Testament is that God exists, that He is Almighty (Pantokrator), and that He is also willing to intervene and to save.

God's willingness to save was manifested when He intervened to free the small nation of ancient Israel from the bondage of mighty Egypt; when He intervened to set free the same people from the Babylonian captivity. Ancient Israel served as a paradigm of God's concern for mankind's salvation.

In the Old Testament the existence of God is taken for granted. There is no groping and searching after God, no questioning, because God progressively reveals Himself. Only "the fool says . . . 'there is no God' " (Ps. 14:1), only those lacking in understanding may speak like "foolish women" (Job 2:10). "The assumption that God exists is the Old Testament's greatest gift to mankind" in the words of Dr. Ludwig Köhler, a leading Old Testament scholar. But the Old Testament also relates the story of the development of monotheism, which might have been inherited from ancient Egypt.

For many centuries, the religion of ancient Israel was not monotheistic but monolatrous. It did not deny the existence of many gods, but it stressed the worship of the tribal god Yahweh. For centuries there were numerous Israelites who believed in gods other than Yahweh. Even though many Jews in Jesus' day considered Moses the father of monotheism, the religion introduced by Moses did not prevail until many centuries later, and it went through several stages of development. As late as the middle of the sixth century before Christ there were numerous Israelites who worshipped Canaanite deities. The worship of other foreign gods was also common, as the chastisements by prophets such as Jeremiah, Second Isaiah, and Ezekiel indicate.

It needs to be said that Old Testament religion did not begin by sweeping aside all former experiences, customs, regulations, practices, and rituals, replacing them with a complete new system of beliefs and values. Whether of Egyptian, Babylonian, or Hellenic origins, experiences and inheritances from the past, were assimilated and many were even left undisturbed. As is the case with other traditions, religions are conditioned by cultural circumstances, established practices, and customs.

It was especially after the fifth century B.C. that monotheism and Yahweh's dominion over all nations was acknowledged by ancient Israel. By the time of Jesus, the conception of Yahweh as the tribal god of Israel had given place to the conception of a universal god, an absolute and holy being. However, during the period in which Palestine was under Hellenistic rule and influence, God was also known as Wisdom, as in the book of Proverbs—wisdom either as a personification or as an attribute of God. This conception is attributed to the influence of Greek thought, which had made its appearance in Palestine nearly one hundred years earlier than the writing of the book of Proverbs.

There were other major influences of Greek thought on post-exilic Judaism. For example, ancient Hebrew religion did not believe in eternal life, and the earliest teaching of life after death is found in the Book of Daniel (12:2–3), written during the Hellenistic period (most probably in the second century). Even at the time of Jesus there were many among the Jews, such as the Sadducees, who did not believe in life after death.

While for many centuries the influence of Hebrew religion on the outside world was minimal, if not totally absent, by the time of Christ it had come to exert a considerable influence, primarily through the Greek-speaking Jews of the diaspora. Emphasis on monotheism, expectation of divine intervention, a desire for liberation from physical as well as spiritual bondage were some of the contributions of Hebrew religion during the Hellenistic period. Alexandrian, or Philonian, Judaism in particular, which had reconciled Jewish faith with such Greek philosophy and thought as that of Platonism, greatly determined the nature and evolution of early Christianity. For many centuries Jewish exclusiveness, and the emphasis on its traditional and legalistic approach, had cut off the ancient Israelites from intellectual intercourse with the "Gentile" world. Following the conquests of Alexander the Great and the wide dissemination of Hellenism (its language, philosophy, outlook) in the Near and the Middle East, there was an intensive interaction between religious beliefs, outlooks, and cultures. For nearly four hundred years Judaism absorbed much from Hellenism, but at the same time its ethical monotheism impressed many in the Mediterranean world. Whether or not one accepts it as an act of providence, the fact is that in addition to Hebrew monotheism, a "new pagan religion . . . was emerging toward the end of antiquity," characterized by "monotheism, the belief in supernatural power, and an antipathy for matter" in the words of Dr. Frederick C. Grant, an American patriarch of Biblical studies and an authority on the Hellenistic world. Monotheism among the philosophers of ancient Greece began developing during the sixth century B.C., with the Ionian philosophers, and assumed momentum with Anaxagoras, Protagoras, and Socrates. Thus Hebrew ethical monotheism and Greek philosophical monotheism supplemented each other and contributed to the cause of early Christianity.

Old Testament religion has been accepted as propaedeutic to Christian theology because it looks forward to a fulfillment, to the time when no longer through prophets and messengers but through God's own appearance would redemption be achieved. The New Testament literature clearly reveals that it starts from the point where the Old Testament ends. "The law [of Moses] and the prophets were until John [the Baptist]," Jesus said (Lk. 16:16). Jesus Christ is constantly seen as the fulfillment of Old Testament prophecy and expectation. In the opening chapter of the Gospel According to Saint Mark we read that "Jesus came into Galilee, preaching the gospel of God, and saying 'The time is fulfilled, and the kingdom of God is at hand' " (Mk. 1:14–15). In the incarnation "the whole fulness of the deity" dwelled bodily in Christ, (Col. 2:9). Saint Paul writes that "when the time had fully come, God sent forth his Son, born of woman, born under the law, . . . so that we might receive adoption as sons" (Gal. 4:4–5).

That Christ was received as the fulfillment of Old Testament prophecy is confirmed by many other passages of the New Testament. Christ's own testimony was that He did not come to destroy the old law but to fulfill it (see Mt. 5:17–48, Lk. 24:44). The early Christian community had no hesitation in seeing the Old Testament events as signposts to the event of the incarnation of God. The Greek Orthodox Church has incorporated this view into its doctrine and liturgical life. In one of the hymns the Church sings: "Let us sound the cymbals: let us shout aloud in songs. The revelation of Christ is now made manifest: the preachings of the prophets have received their fulfillment . . ." And elsewhere:

Hearken, O heaven, and give ear, O earth. Let the foundations be shaken, and let trembling lay hold upon the neth-
ermost parts of the world. For our God and Creator has
clothed himself in created flesh, and He who with His strong
arm fashioned the creation reveals Himself in the womb of
her that He formed. Oh the depth of the riches of the wisdom
and knowledge of God! How unsearchable are His judg-
ments, and His ways past finding out!

In the encounter between Hellenism and Judaism, it was
Judaism that was destined to adopt the Greek language and
thought, Greek manners and habits. It was on the evidence
that the greatest part of later Judaism was Hellenized that scholars, such as J. G. Droysen and F. Altheim, defend the theory
that Christianity was nearer to Hellenism than Judaism. At any
rate, by the time that Jesus Christ was born, Judaism and Hellenism were forces that were not opposed in principle.

Early Christianity as well as modern Greek Orthodox Christianity accepts the person of Jesus Christ as the point of con-
vergence between Hebraic prophecy and Hellenic expectation.
This is eloquently expressed in another Greek Orthodox
Church hymn:

Of Old Habakkuk the prophet was counted worthy to behold
ineffably the figure and symbol of Christ's birth, and he fore-
told in song the renewal of mankind. For a young child, even
the Logos [Word], has now come forth from the Mountain
[see Daniel 2:45], that is the Virgin, unto the renewal of the
peoples. . . .

Thus, in addition to the religious phenomenon (the evolution
of civilization as a whole) and the Hebraic religious heritage,
the Greek Orthodox view Ancient Greek (or Hellenic) philosophy and religious beliefs as a preparation (propaedeia) for
Christianity. The heritage of Hellenism is received both directly, from the Greek sources, and indirectly, through Hellenistic Judaism.

The Heritage of Hellenism

At the time when Christ was born, the people of the Mediterranean world were under Roman rule. Rome had achieved
what the Greeks had failed to achieve, namely political unity.

But long before the establishment of Roman rule, the Greeks had achieved the cultural unity of the Mediterranean world and even of lands beyond it. The conquest of the Persian Empire (including Syria, Palestine, Egypt) and of all western Asia to the Indus River by Alexander the Great established in that part of the world a widespread knowledge of the Greek language and of Greek ideas, and a Greek outlook and orientation. Modern Biblical scholars and historians of the Hellenistic and Roman worlds confirm that Greek influence was both widespread and profound. Frederick C. Grant, mentioned earlier, writes:

> Only scattered pockets of non-Greek culture, language, and religion survived here and there. . . . Everyone could read— or very nearly everyone; most men could write. Even day-labourers in the dockyards and on the quays and in the grain warehouses knew Greek and could converse in the language of Homer, Plato, Aristotle—even though they did not often converse like them.

Even centuries before Alexander's conquests the influence of Hellenism in the Near East had been widespread. In recent years, there have been excavations of Greek colonies of the middle of the seventh century and following.

> The remains of ancient Graeco-Roman cities, with their Hellenistic architecture and sculpture, are found in both Syria and Egypt, and in Palestine as well; the inscriptions, the books produced there, the thousands of papyrus letters and other documents written in Greek, which have been found buried in the dry sands of Egypt—all this evidence proves how highly Hellenized that part of the world was, especially after the second century before Christ

to quote again from Grant's outstanding work *Roman Hellenism and the New Testament*. The penetration of the language, religion, philosophy, and other aspects of Greek life had been achieved much earlier in the Roman west. Rome itself had long been a bilingual city. Several Latin authors, including Pliny, Tacitus, Cicero, Juvenal, and Horace, attest to the heavy Hellenization of the Latin west, which can be traced back to the eighth century—if not earlier.

Despite political unity, the bulk of society under Rome lived under difficult conditions, the result of civil wars, injustices in the social order, the large number of slaves, and the failure of the state to satisfy the religious and spiritual needs of the ordinary people. The overwhelming majority of the urban populations and the large numbers of serfs attached to great estates yearned for *soteria* (redemption, security, salvation). What must I do to be saved? (cf Mk. 10:17, Lk. 18:18) was a question of common concern. Christianity promised to offer what other systems had failed to provide.

Christianity, of course, began as a movement within Palestinian Judaism, but within a few years it was transformed from a Palestinian Jewish creed into a universal religion. Why? What contributed to that transformation? There are two very important phenomena that reveal the process of transformation.

As has already been indicated, Palestine, though a Roman province at the time of Christ, had been heavily Hellenized, and for more than three hundred and fifty years the impact of Hellenism on Judaism was deep. The Hellenized Jews—not only those of the upper classes, but many ordinary folk, such as some of the disciples of Christ—spoke and wrote in Greek. Parts of their Holy Scriptures had been translated into Greek as early as the first quarter of the third century (the complete Hebrew Old Testament was translated into Greek between 285 and 150 B.C.). Some of the Old Testament books that made up a second canon (known by the Orthodox as deuterocanonical) were written directly in Greek. With very few exceptions, there was no complaint against Hellenism. In the words of Dr. Moses Hadas of Columbia University: "In the Near East a segment (but only a segment) of the Jewish people resisted the Hellenism which their near neighbors welcomed." The Jews were enmeshed in the political, economic, social, and cultural implications of the Hellenic presence in Judaea. It has been rightly observed by Dr. F. E. Peters of New York University that since Judaism met Hellenism Jewish thought has never been the same.

Other leading scholars of the period are equally convinced that the presence of Hellenism in Palestine was not only widespread but also profound. Dr. Victor Tcherikover, a professor at the Hebrew University in Jerusalem, writes that the thirty Greek cities, with Greek populations, in Jewish Palestine proper had great influence thoughout all of Palestine. The Greek cities in Palestine and Syria, and elsewhere in the Near East, were like the Greek cities (the *poleis*) of antiquity, "for a Greek city could neither be created nor strike root in the country unless Greeks came to it," in the words of Dr. Tcherikover. The Greeks, of course, didn't confine themselves within their cities, but communicated with the outside world through commerce and trade, agriculture, and the crafts. Their cities, like the *poleis* of classical time, became centers of Greek learning and civilization. The Hellenization of the Jews was a voluntary self-Hellenization, like the self-Americanization of American Jews, Italians, Greeks, and others.

Dr. Martin Hengel, of the University of Tübingen, is the author of several important studies, including a monumental two-volume work on Judaism and Hellenism. He indicates that Hellenization was so widespread in Jewish Palestine that we should not speak of Palestinian Judaism but only of Hellenistic Judaism. To speak of Palestinian Judaism is to "pass too lightly over the fact that by the time of Jesus, Palestine had already been under Hellenistic rule and its resultant cultural influence for some 360 years." He goes on to explain that in Palestine "Hellenistic civilization was by no means an exclusively or even predominantly military, civic and socio-economic phenomenon—these were simply the areas in which its effects first became visible; rather, it was the expression of a force which embraced almost every sphere of life. It was . . . an expression of the power of the Greek spirit which penetrated and shaped everything, expressive and receptive."

Several other leading scholars of the period, such as Nigel Turner, J. N. Sevenster, Moshe Schwabe, and Baruch Lifshitz, have demonstrated that the Greek language and Hellenistic culture were not restricted to the upper classes in Palestine but had permeated all circles of Jewish society. On the basis of inscriptions alone, Schwabe and Lifshitz, both of the Hebrew University in Jerusalem, conclude that "anyone who has examined the Greco-Jewish inscriptions in Palestine, including those of Beth She' arim, is well aware that . . . Greek was used by the Jews in general and not only by the intellectuals and city dwellers among them."

As Judaism did not resist Hellenization, likewise Christianity did not reject the mind, the philosophy, the language, the style of life, or even the politics of Hellenism. In fact, Christianity did not seek to destroy but to consecrate it. Christianity and Greco-Roman culture were not two independent, antithetical entities, each with its own spiritual vision. Early Christianity and later medieval catholic Christianity never saw a sharp dichotomy between Christian faith and Greco-Roman culture. Early Christian authors such as Justin, Clement of Alexandria, Origen, and many more slowly developed a deliberate synthesis of the two. Christianity appeared not as a reaction against Greek classical philosophy but as a new spiritual force, which united the Greek and Roman world with the religious impulse of the Semitic Near East, with the Jewish Scriptures in particular.

Greek thought served as a *propaedeia*, a preparation for Christian doctrines. For example, the doctrine of God was formulated on the basis of centuries-old Greek intellectual tradition. The debate in the early Church about the nature of God, God as the "enclosing," not the "enclosed," traces back to pre-Socratic philosophy, even though it derived much more from Aristotle's discussion of the infinite. When Christian intellectuals such as Hermas, Theophilos, Athenagoras, Irenaios, Gregory of Nazianzos, and Gregory of Nyssa spoke of God as the *chorōn* (the one who contains all things) and asserted that God alone is *achōretos* (uncontained), they used Greek philosphical categories proposed by Xenophanes, Plato, and Aristotle. Church Fathers used Greek philosophy not only to attack polytheism but also to explain Old Testament anthropomorphism.

Many elements claimed by Christianity as uniquely Christian can be found in ancient Greek as well as in other religions. Divine revelation, for example, was not limited to ancient Israel, and it cannot be claimed as an element unique to the Christian religion. Natural revelation is a very important element in several religions. The ancient Greeks, for example, believed that man's knowledge derived from God. Protagoras, Xenophanes, and the tragedians spoke many religious truths. Xenophanes writes that "truly the gods have not revealed to mortals all things from the beginnings; but mortals by long seeking discover what is better." This view, which assigns progress and evolution to man, was stated in similar and indeed in more concrete terms by Aeschylos and Sophocles. The religion of the ancient Greeks at a certain stage of its development was polytheistic, but under the influence of their great intellectuals they conceived the idea of one God. At no time were the ancient Greeks uniform in their religious beliefs and practices. They were eclectic. There was no canon, no "Bible," no codified decree that forced them into religious uniformity. Not without justification the Church Fathers observed centuries later that many heresies in the early church had originated in the free spirit of Hellenism (many other heresies were of Jewish and Oriental origins). "Heresy," from the Greek *haeresis,* means choice, and the Greeks exercised the right of choice.

While some ancient Greeks were polytheists, others were monotheists. Some took the Olympian gods very seriously; others saw God everywhere and identified God with life. Nature was nothing but life, spirit, the divinity itself. Some worshipped statues while others saw in statues only an image of the deity, not the deity itself. Creation as a whole, including human life, was sanctified by the presence of the divinity, which revealed itself in diverse ways, in nature as well as in human consciousness. It was for this reason that they erected altars, temples, and statues everywhere, reminding themselves of the divinity's omnipresence. There is little doubt that the deepest foundation of religious feeling in the ancient Greek world was the mysterious life of nature, a life infused with spirit, and also with divinity. Life in ancient Greece was all-encompassing and it encompassed organic and inorganic nature. Dead nature did not exist. Meadows and forests, springs and rivers, lakes and seas, measureless space, and silent mountain ranges were equally divine.

Ancient Greek literature (poetry, drama, history) reveals that the Greeks were not only devoutly religious but that they believed in the universality of religion. In Homer's *Odyssey* we read that Nestor's son Pisistratos tells Telemachos at Pylos that "all men stand in need of gods." The Greeks were conscious of the weaknesses and the limitations of humanity, which induce human beings to depend on a power or powers higher than themselves. The Greeks reveal more than once their longing for God's love and protection from the evils of the world, from natural catastrophes, from pestilences and illnesses. Thus in ancient Greek life "all things are full of the gods," as Thales of Miletos and Plato taught.

The historian Xenophon relates that Klearchos, in a conversation with the traitor Tissaphernes, states that "all things in all places are subject to the gods, and all alike the gods hold in their control." The Christian teaching that "God became man that man might become God" has its parallels in Greek religion and philosophy. The sixth-century philosopher Heraklitos writes that "mortals are immortals and immortals are mortals, living the immortals' death and dying the immortals' life." It is no wonder then that every Greek town had more temples, shrines, and sacred groves than a Christian medieval city had churches. It is a well-known fact that Greek religion had a permanent influence on the beliefs, rituals, theology, and ethics of Christianity. When Greek religion and Christianity met, they were fused, and after their fusion many of the older forms and beliefs reappeared under different forms.

There are numerous chapels and altars in modern Greece, as in antiquity, in honor of Christ, His Mother, His apostles, and His saints. As a statue did not become an object of worship before its consecration, an icon today does not become the object of veneration if it has not been consecrated. As the statue in antiquity was, for the educated and the enlightened, only the image of the deity, likewise today the icons of the Orthodox are images and abstract representations of the virtues of the divine beings. As images and rites were the guides of religious feeling, likewise icons and rituals are the most potent medium of religious feeling among the Orthodox today.

As we have already indicated, the ancient Greeks considered their religion as revealed. It had its prophets and its theophanies, such as Melampos, Orpheus, Hesiod, Musaeos, Epimenides, Pythagoras, Empedocles, and Socrates, and the Eleusinian, Bacchic, and Orphic mysteries. They had their nympholepts, that is, prophets who had received their divine gifts of prophecy and insight from the nymphs, the daughters of the Great

Mother Earth. Socrates viewed himself as a gift of God to the Athenians, as a gadfly to stir them to higher things. In his famous apology, which was recorded by Plato, Socrates stressed that his mission was divine. "I am that gadfly which God has attached to the state, and all day long and in all places am always fastening upon you, arousing and persuading and reproaching you." Without Socrates the Athenians "would sleep on for the remainder of their lives, unless God in his care" should send them another gadfly.

Notwithstanding its diversity, Greek religious thought was both serious and profound. The nineteenth-century German classical scholar and philologist Erwin Rhode writes, with some exaggeration perhaps, that "both the deepest and the boldest thoughts about divinity arose in ancient Greece." Because of their religious quests and the variety of their religious experiences, the ancient Hellenes have been described by the greatest classical scholar of the late nineteenth and early twentieth centuries, Ulrich von Wilamowitz-Moellendorff, as "the most devout nation of the world."

As early as the sixth century B.C., there were Greeks who believed in one God who reigned supreme above all gods and mortals. To quote again the philosopher Xenophanes, "one God there is, greatest of gods and men." Other thinkers believed that names such as Apollo, Zeus, Dionysos, and others were different names for the same deity, who functions in diverse ways and assumes a different name according to the occasion.

Greek monotheism developed progressively after the sixth century. A treatise that has survived under the name of Aristotle states that "God, being one, yet has many names, being called after all the various conditions which he himself inaugurates." The chief characteristic of the one God is that of providence and concern over the cosmos or the creation. In later Greek, non-Christian thought, Dio Chrysostom and Maximos Tyrios expressed belief in monotheism in more concrete terms. Maximos proclaimed "There is one God, king and father of all."

Though Greek thought after the sixth century before the Christian Era emphasized man's ability to work creatively upon his environment and to assert himself over and against a hostile or indifferent cosmos, rationalistic views did not always obtain, and humanity was often seen as in the bondage of *hamartia* (sin) or subject to uncontrollable limitations. Knowledge, intelligence, power, and material wealth were not considered unambiguously good.

It is primarily the realm of the divine that defines the boundaries of what the human being can know and do. Where the human realm ends the divine begins. Human knowledge and human power and responsibilities are, of course, limited. To try to overstep the boundary line between the human and the divine brings on serious consequences. Thinkers like Socrates and Sophocles made the distinction between the man-made and the natural, between the temporal and the eternally existent. They conceptualized the issues of divine versus human law, the individual versus the community, private versus public morality, religious versus secular values. The Greeks spoke of certain absolutes which "live always," and for the most part they rejected autocratic rationalism and crushing materialism. The divine and the human, the physical and the metaphysical world, fused and remained interrelated through the Greek intellectual tradition. It is sinful (*hamartima*) to violate not only the divine, but also the relations between man and nature.

Certainly the Greeks emphasized the greatness of the human being, but that greatness was measured against the subjugated natural world, not the divine law, which manifests itself in many ways both in the internal and in the external world of man. While both the world of man and the world of nature are not helpless, neither are they all-powerful and supreme. In general the ancient Greeks struck a balance between the physical and the metaphysical. God or the gods punish only those who commit *hybris* against the divine or against fellow human beings—not those with *eusebia* (reverence) and humility (*autognosia*).

To violate divine law is sinful, and to devalue the human is not only an insult (*hybris*) to humanity but also a brutalization of human relationships with the divine. Several ancient Greek thinkers stressed that there are areas of existence that cannot or should not be subjected to the control, coercion, or authority of man. While the human, the physical world, and the nonhuman, the metaphysical, are inseparably linked, the human is subject to the metaphysical realm, which lies beyond man's control.

In Greek thought, as in the *Antigone* and *Oedipus at Kolonos* of Sophocles, even death, that "heroic acceptance of the unknown," bears witness to man's dignity and to divine promises. To live humanly was to know fully the strengths and limitations of man's existence; to die was both an assertion of man's humanity and an acceptance of God or the gods and their limitless, ageless, and unbending conditions. Knowledge of man's human qualities involved recognition of the unyielding factuality of the divine—the only "things that are."

Man's progressive knowledge of things divine is also seen in Greek anthropological thought. On the whole it stressed belief in the dignity and infinite worth of the human person, which personified the heavenly God upon earth. Man's energy was viewed as the embodiment of the vital energy of the gods. He was considered a microcosm of the visible and the invisible, the natural and the supernatural. Man's mind or soul was respected as a miniature world that expressed its vision in art and thought, imagination and remembrance, goodness, beauty, and truth, conceiving and re-creating reality.

As a result of the influence of ancient Greek thought and its concept of natural revelation, there is in Orthodox thought today no opposition between the human and the natural, no separating of reason and faith, spirituality and materiality. The natural, or "secular," is sanctified in the whole realm of God's creation. Thus the Orthodox believe that human life and the universe require unity and equilibrium, and they observe in their theology a balance between faith and reason, logic and sentiment, natural and supernatural revelation, belief and conduct.

It must be noted that monotheism in the ancient Greek world, which was never absolute, was practiced primarily by philosophers and thinkers, while polytheism was widely practiced by the common folk.

Nevertheless the influence of ancient Greek religion on Christian religion, as demonstrated by such prominent scholars and students of ancient Greek religion as Thaddeus Zielinski and Martin P. Nilsson, is apparent in every major aspect of Christianity, its doctrine, ethics, and worship. It is not without reason that Christianity has been described as very syncretic. While Christian theology, philosophy, and ethics have been strongly influenced by Platonism and Stoicism, much Aristotelianism lies behind Christian dialectics, definitions and creeds, theological and creedal categories.

On the popular level, several religious practices of ancient Greek origin have survived in the Greek world. Ancient Greek religious elements appeared in early Christian religiosity in a number of forms, including piety, superstition, demonology, and ritual. It has been rightly observed that "when Christianity adopted the pagan basilica, it took over much of its furniture and practices."

The survival of Greek religious practices in Christian religiosity is confirmed by several Church canons, commentaries on canons, liturgical services and prayers, lives of saints, and other sources, including historical accounts.

To be sure, attempts were made to eradicate persistent practices of ancient Greek religion, but without success. Many of them have remained extant to the present day. The great number of religious services, prayers, exorcisms, and blessings of the Orthodox Church indicate that in its evolution the Church consecrated the whole of life—mind and body, logic and senses, feelings, and whatever constitutes human life.

In the area of Christian mysticism, the influence of Greek religious mysticism is no less apparent. The teaching concerning *theosis* (deification) is a good illustration. According to early and medieval Christian theology, the ultimate goal of the faithful is to achieve *theosis*—eternal life in God—not, however, absorbed by God in a pantheistic manner. Early as well as later Greek Fathers of the Middle Ages made much use of this concept. *Theosis* became synonymous with salvation, and salvation was the presence of the human in God, while damnation was the absence of God from the life of the human. Saint Irenaios put it in the following manner: "In His unfathomable love, God became what we are, that He might make us what He is."

The idea of *theosis* was not foreign to the classical Greek mind. It was associated with *philosophia*, with *paideia* through philosophical exercise (*ascesis*) and intellectual growth, rather than with a religious experience, as was the case in the Christian tradition. For Greek thought, philosophy is the path, the *anabasis*, the ascent to *theosis*. Plato was quite emphatic. In writing about the just man, Plato says that God will not neglect the righteous man, the man who "by the practice of virtue is to be likened unto God so far as that is possible for man." Some of Plato's teaching is echoed in the writings of the Neoplatonists, for instance Ammonios of Alexandria: "Philosophy is likeness in God so far as that is possible for man [*philosophia esti omoiosis theo kata to dynaton anthropo*]." And the fourth-century philosopher and rhetorician Themistios repeats that "philosophy is nothing else than assimilation to God to the extent that it is possible for man."

The Greek influence on the early Christians was not only that of the thought-world of the Greeks, their religious and philosophical heritage, but also that of their mythology and of symbols from their culture and social realities, as sociologists like Peter Berger, Thomas Luckman, and Mary Douglas have emphasized. Even Greek tragedy was emulated in the Christian gospel. For example, Gilbert Bilezikian writes that Mark incorporated elements of the Greek dramatic literary form that prevailed in the cultural milieu of his time. Bilezikian adds that even though Mark did not intend to write a Greek tragedy, he used all the distinctive dramatic features of Greek tragedy to convey a powerful gospel message.

In the area of ethics one wonders where Greek ethical principles end and where Christian ethics start. For example, the ethical teachings of early Christian writers are remarkably similar to those of non-Christian thinkers. On subjects such as love, hate, money, family, and society, Plutarch, the Greek moralist and biographer, and early Christian literature express very similar notions—a fact that can hardly be accidental. Whereas it is improbable that Christian writers knew of Plutarch's writings or vice versa, the answer lies in the common moral background. Both Plutarch and Christian writers came under the influence of the same elements of Greek philosophy, such as Platonism, Aristotelianism, Cynicism, and Stoicism.

How did early Christian authors justify the adoption of Greek culture? They referred to Old Testament precedents. For example, the great theologian Origen of Alexandria cited the "spoliation of the Egyptians" by the Hebrews (Ex. 12:35–36) in order to justify the Christians' own expropriation of the thought-world of pagan Hellenism. According to the Exodus account, when they left Egypt the Hebrews made off with the gold and silver ornaments of the Egyptians. Likewise, following the example of the ancient Israelites, the Christians took over the wisdom and culture of ancient Hellenism.

Christians need not apologize because their religion has inherited so much from the Greek philosophical and religious thought of antiquity. As Socrates, the fourth-century Church historian, writes: "The good wherever it is found is a property of the truth." The Orthodox Church believes that every effort made by the human spirit in its pursuit of reality and truth is of perennial worth. In the course of the centuries Christianity has not destroyed the past but adopted and consecrated it. It is as impossible to de-Hellenize Christianity as it is to de-Orientalize Judaism. The purity of Judaism is a myth and the purity of Christianity is a myth. Both have inherited from several sources. It has been rightly observed that "Greek religion and philosophy did not entirely vanish from the consciousness of the Christianized world: it penetrated into it, it lives in it to this day, and will live so long as Christianity itself shall live." Early Christianity accommodated itself to the prevailing thought-forms and cultural values of the society in which it found itself. The Church in her effort to spread the Christian gospel meaningfully exploited the thought of the Greco-Roman world as well as that of other societies.

To be sure, there was hostility to Hellenic thought, religious practices, and culture. But ultimately it was the Hellenized school of Christian theology and the synthesis achieved by the Cappadocian Fathers that prevailed. The edicts of Theodosios the Great in the fourth century and of Justinian in the sixth, the temper of monasticism, several Church canons, and the efforts of certain patriarchs did not succeed in destroying Greek religious thought and culture. As the eminent British scholar William Ralph Inge writes: "A doctrine or custom is not necessarily un-Christian because it is Greek or pagan. I know of no stranger perversity than for men who rest the whole weight of their religion upon history, to suppose that our Lord meant to raise an universal religion on a purely Jewish basis." Inge adds that "Christianity conquered Hellenism by borrowing from it all its best elements; and I do not see that a Christian need feel any reluctance to make this admission." But in the process Christianity conquered and transformed Hellenism as well. The aspirations of the ancient world, the Messianic expectations of ancient Israel, and the philosophical and religious quests of the Greeks, Romans, Syrians, and others, converged in the person of Christ. As the author of the Epistle to the Hebrews writes: "In many and various ways God spoke of old to our fathers by the prophets; but in these last days he has spoken to us in the Son, whom he appointed the heir of all things, through whom also he created the world. He reflects the glory of God and bears the very stamp of his nature, upholding the universe by his word of power" (Heb. 1:1–3).

Christianity: The Fullness of Time

I indicated above that from an Orthodox viewpoint, Christianity emerged as the fulfillment not only of Old Testament prophecy and ancient Hebrew expectation, but also of the history of mankind, and that of the ancient Mediterranean world in particular. Apostolic Fathers such as Ignatios of Antioch; apologists such as Justin Martyr; ecclesiastical and theological writers of great influence such as Clement of Alexandria, Origen, and Eusebios of Caesarea; major Church Fathers of the fourth and fifth centuries, including Basil the Great, Gregory of Nyssa, Augustine of Hippo—all perceived Christianity as the religion that began with the creation of the world. The Logos doctrine of John's Gospel, which identifies Divine Reason (Logos, or "Word") with Christ, sees Christ as God existing before all creation and revealing Himself progressively in "various ways and diverse manners."

Christianity is the religion in which the person and the teachings of Christ occupy the central position. Christ removed the discord between God and man. And this removal of discord is made possible by and functions through the religious fellow-ship (*koinonia*) known as the Ecclesia (Church), of which He remains the Head. Thus the right relation of man to God is reestablished. Christianity is the most complete revelation of God to man in the person of Him who is both God and man, a *theanthropos,* who was ever God from eternity, and man from the moment of His conception in the womb of the Virgin Mary.

The central affirmation of Christianity is that Jesus Christ, who is God and eternally both transcendent and immanent, became a human being in order to take human beings back into God's fold, and that by His death and resurrection He has become the source of forgiveness of sin, newness of life, re-demption, and eternal life in God—otherwise known as *theosis.* God's concern and love for human beings prompted the in-carnation and is expressed through the Church, her life of prayer, faith, and the sacraments instituted by Christ Himself or by His early disciples under the direction of the Holy Spirit.

Of course Christian truth cannot be "proved" in the way that a mathematical equation can be solved. Christianity is a way of life. Christianity is itself faith and inner life and experience: These are its bases, not necessarily research, intellectual thought, and logic, even though logic and thought are not foreign to the Christian mind.

As the founder of Christianity appeared to His contempo-raries to be an extraordinary person, likewise Christianity's early history is most unusual. Christ appeared as a unique per-sonality in human history. His birth has been accepted as a miracle and His life as an enigma. At the age of thirty He appeared as a man claiming to be the Son of God and the Savior of humankind. He lived among men "doing good." Of His thirty-three years on earth, He spent only three active years in public life. However, those three years were time enough to revolutionize the whole world and establish a new order. Every aspect of Western civilization bears the mark of His influence.

Christ is the Lord of a billion people all over the world today. His ideals triumphed through peaceful teaching and practical philanthropy. For over three hundred years, Christianity had no official status in the Roman Empire. During most of that time, membership in the Church—that is, in the community of Christ's followers—was in fact a criminal offence. Widespread and incredibly brutal persecutions were not uncommon, but the Christians did not respond to violence with violence. They blessed their persecutors, they prayed for the men who released wild animals against them and who burned them alive. But an empire was conquered, not by swords and trampling armies, but by faith, hope in the life to come, and the practice of love and philanthropy among themselves and toward others. The strong convictions and "good works" of the martyrs were truly the seeds of the Christian Ecclesia. Christianity made converts of all races and classes of people and became a universal religion.

Christ's mission on earth was continued by His followers—the twelve Apostles, later the seventy disciples, the three and the five thousands, the people that made up "the Church." It is this Church that is the agency through which God's will is carried out. This community of people proclaimed that "there is salvation in no one else, for there is no other name under heaven given among men by which we must be saved" (Acts 4:12). Even today, Christians everywhere believe that Christ is that final revelation of religion for which the human soul longs. In His incarnation, the event of God made man, the history of ancient Israel and the quests of the Greek and Roman worlds, as well as the gropings of all mankind, were fulfilled. Because of the Christ event "secular" history was transformed into "sacred" history.

Christianity became the most influential religion in the history of Western civilization. At least for fifteen centuries it was the faith, the concern, and the way of life for millions of people. Literature, art, history, government, and other areas of human endeavor have been greatly influenced by the Christian faith and ideal. Early Christianity was characterized by "unity in diversity." But in the course of centuries this unity was broken under the pressure of human circumstances to the extent that today we speak of four major divisions in the Christian religion: Greek, or Eastern, Orthodox Christianity; Roman Catholicism; Protestantism; and Oriental Orthodox Christianity (the faith of the Lesser Churches of the Near East: Coptic, Armenian, Nestorian, and others). For conventional and practical purposes we may speak of three major events that brought about these divisions in the body of Christianity. The theological efforts of the fifth century to define Christian doctrine and the decisions of the Council of Chalcedon (451) contributed to the first serious schism between the "Lesser Churches" of the Near East and Orthodox Catholic, or "Chalcedonian," Christianity. Events in medieval Christendom, from the ninth to the twelfth century, contributed to the second and more serious schism between Greek and Roman Christianity, which became a reality after 1204, with the Fourth Crusade and the sacking of Constantinople by the Crusaders. Finally events within Roman, or Western, Catholic Christianity in the fifteenth and sixteenth centuries contributed to the genesis of Protestant Christianity in several different forms. The year of Martin Luther's protest in 1517 became the starting point of the Reformation movement.

Serious differences among all four branches of Christianity exist; but there are more things that unite Christians than things that divide them. They all believe in one God, they all acknowledge one Lord, they all accept one baptism, they all have the same Bible. The ecumenical movement of the last thirty years aims at the restoration of Christian unity, a unity in obedience to Christ's commands of brotherly love (Jn. 15:17) and of complete unity (Jn. 17:22–23). Only through the fraternal love and the perfect unity of its followers will Christianity be able to challenge the world to recognize its values and its claims.

2

The Faith
of Greek Orthodoxy

W hat is the doctrinal content of Greek Orthodoxy and
what exactly does an Orthodox Christian believe? At
the outset it should be stated that an Orthodox Christian believes that he is a living member of, and in organic unity with,
the original Church. In every Sunday or weekday liturgy the
following declaration of faith is made by the faithful:

> I believe in one God, Father Almighty, Maker of Heaven and
> Earth and of everything visible and invisible. And in one
> Lord Jesus Christ, the only begotten son of God, begotten
> of the Father before all ages. Light of Light, True God of
> True God, begotten not made, consubstantial with the Father,
> through whom all things were made. Who for us human
> beings and for our salvation came down from heaven, and
> was incarnate by the Holy Spirit and of the Virgin Mary, and
> became Man. He was crucified for our salvation under Pon-
> tius Pilate. He suffered, died and was buried, and was res-
> urrected on the third day according to the Scriptures. And
> ascended into heaven and sat at the right hand of the Father;
> and He will return in glory to judge the living and the dead;
> Whose reign will have no end. And I believe in the Holy
> Spirit, the Lord, the Giver of Life; who proceeds from the
> Father; who together with the Father and the Son is wor-
> shipped and glorified; who spoke through the Prophets. I
> believe in one, holy, catholic and apostolic Church. I ac-
> knowledge one baptism for the forgiveness of sins. I await
> the resurrection of the dead, and the life of the ages to come.

This is the faith of the Orthodox Church in its briefest form. It was long the faith of undivided Christendom (at least until the eleventh century), formulated by the deliberations of the representatives of all Christendom in the two great ecumenical synods of Nicaea (325) and Constantinople (381). It is known as the symbol of faith, or the Nicene Creed.

The essence of the creed can be rendered in one sentence: God is revealed in Jesus Christ, and man is redeemed by Jesus Christ. God manifested Himself in time and space to redeem man and reconcile him with Himself. "God was made man that man may become God," as Saint Athanasios put it. The Son of God, Jesus Christ, became incarnate in order to renew man and make him a new creation through the Holy Spirit, "the Giver of Life."

Man is expected to become a new creature within the Church, which is the totality of those who believe and live in Christ, who are attached to the visible body of Christ (who remains its head) like living cells in a living organism. Church members are animated by the common means of sanctification: common worship, the sacraments, the reading of the Word of God, and a life of spiritual growth and development. The Orthodox Church insists on constant communion with God, on prayer and spirituality. The believer is sustained and guarded by the conscience of the Church, which is the supreme authority in Orthodoxy, an authority that rests on the totality of the faithful, lay persons and clergymen alike.

The Orthodox Christian is expected to abide by the teachings of Christ. Love and charity, justice and self-knowledge (*autognosia*), which means constant repentance and renewal—these are emphasized in the Greek Orthodox Church. The ethics of the Greek Orthodox are Christ-centered. Right belief and right conduct (*orthodoxia* and *orthopraxia*) constitute the two poles of the Christian axis. Neither faith alone, nor conduct nor law alone.

The creed cited above speaks of baptism, of forgiveness of sins, and other mysterious truths not subject to experimentation or even logic. The Orthodox Church has "mysteries," which correspond to what Western Christianity calls "sacraments." There are many mysteries in Christianity: for example the mystery of faith, the doctrine of the Holy Trinity, the belief in two perfect natures of Christ, the procession of the Holy Spirit, redemption, and the like. But by "mysteries" the Church means specific services that convey grace given by God directly or indirectly to his Church through the Holy Spirit, who penetrates every aspect of man's life.

Through these mysteries or sacraments, the regenerating, justifying, sanctifying, and redemptive grace of God is bestowed upon the faithful.

The God of the Orthodox

The first article of the Orthodox creed—"I believe in one God, Father Almighty, Maker of Heaven and Earth and of everything visible and invisible"—assumes, and at the same time implicitly raises the question of, the existence of God. Can the existence of God be proved? Orthodoxy believes that the existence of God cannot be proved in scientific, philosophical, or theological terms. The proof most people have in mind is experimental proof, where experiments are conducted under controlled conditions. That kind of proof is possible only in a very limited area of investigation.

Some people of course use logic to argue against the existence of God. But logic has its own limitations, for many "logical" proofs get upset by equally logical challenges. The major part of life is outside the sphere of scientific, mathematical, and logical proofs. Honor, justice, loyalty, love, which are among the most powerful forces in life, cannot be proved in any of these ways. As we cannot put any of these values into a test tube, so man cannot put God into a test tube. Much of life proceeds on probabilities and on considerable faith. Belief in God does not rest on argument and is never produced by it. With the heart man believes, and he who does not feel the need of faith cannot be led to it by logic (cf. Rom. 10:10). Frequently, personal experiences cannot be understood in terms of logic. Denial of the existence of God or of a first cause of being leaves more questions unsolved than it seems to solve.

We cannot demonstrate "the being of a god," but we can show that objections to belief in the existence of God are unsound. If the existence of God cannot be proved in a chemistry laboratory or by mathematics or logic, neither can it be disproved. The most learned and militant unbeliever has never been able to state conclusively that the existence of God is impossible. Profound thinkers of all centuries have heard the arguments of the unbelievers or atheists and still believed in God. While people cannot prove the existence of God, they can speak about it through personal experiences. In addition, there are many other indications of the existence of God.

The broad basis of religious belief is, first, the existence of the universe itself and the evidence of design and order in it. The argument that "it just happened" is superficial. We cannot believe that a heap of rubble and stones and marbles thrown upon a hill can by itself turn into a Parthenon, a Hagia Sophia, a Saint Peter's, or an Empire State Building. Likewise we cannot believe that this universe came into being without an architect, or first cause, behind it. The Bible puts it in these words: "Every house is built by some one, but the builder of all things is God" (Heb. 3:4).

Another indication of the existence of God lies in the fact, already noted, that human beings everywhere, in all historical ages, have believed in God. "The knowledge that there is a God was implanted in us by God himself," as Saint John Chrysostom writes.

The voice of conscience or of a natural law within the human being is a voice confirming the existence of God. People are aware of a moral sense within them. The term "ought" and its authoritative command is common to all humanity. People did not need to have commandments in order to know that kindness is better than cruelty, truth better than a lie, and love better than hate. Where did those certainties come from? How could one know them without being told? They are a thumbprint of the great mind that made man. The very fact that one knows that some things are right and some wrong is witness enough that God is not dead, but very much alive.

What is God? The human being can never know what God is. All names used to describe "him," "her," or "it" are anthropomorphic. Only what God is not can be known. He is not what the human being perceives. As Clement of Alexandria writes: "Though we ascribe names [to God], they are not to be taken in their strict meaning; when we call him one, good, mind, existence, father, God, creator, Lord, we are not conferring a name on him."

While the Orthodox believe that God is the creator, they also believe that He is in creation. He permeates all things and all things are within Him. He is not divided or split by creation. Thus mankind lives within God, and God lives within mankind. The human being through its free will and mind achieves a consciousness of God, and realizes its own godliness by elevating this consciousness into faith and into a religious life.

As such, God is omnipresent, and the belief in the existence of the divinity everywhere means that religion is eternally present, bringing time and eternity together, divinizing humanity as well as the whole cosmos. Divinity, whether it goes by the name God, Logos, Beauty, First Mover, or Lord, is perceived as a vast creative force, a dynamic and vital reality, a source of all energy and the primal power behind life, the very essence of intelligence and creativity which permeates every aspect of the universe. Thus, in essence God is dynamic, both transcendent and immanent, within and without the world, the original causation and continuous cosmic presence.

The ideas of the fatherhood of God and the inner experience of God's presence have been common beliefs and experiences of the Greeks as well as of many other people in history. In the Greek experience, religion, instead of being one department of life, has been at the very core of life, the central harmonizing factor of life's various departments—the whole of life is religious and permeated with God's presence.

Nevertheless, all the preceding arguments do not constitute proofs of the existence or the nature of God; they constitute enormous indications. It is to these probabilities that unbelievers, atheists, skeptics, searchers, are urged to turn in order that they may be convinced of the existence of God.

For Orthodox Christians the greatest evidence of the existence and the attributes of God is the historical person of Jesus Christ. "No one has ever seen God; the only Son, who is in the bosom of the Father, he has made him known" (Jn. 1:18). The existence of God and His qualities have been revealed to man by Jesus Christ, who taught that God is a person, in fact the creator of the universe and the father of the human race.

However, the biggest problem is not to believe in a god but to believe in a personal god. People of all historical ages have believed that God in some sense exists, and they have conceived of God as a first cause or a principle of order or an external power. The problem is to think of God in personal terms, as one who actually addresses man and enters into intimate and reciprocal relationships with him, as is the case with the God of the Christian Scriptures.

This personal God is understood as one in essence (*ousia*), but three in persons (*hypostaseis*). The theological and philosophical foundations for the Orthodox understanding of the Trinity were laid in the discussions and formulations of the fourth and the fifth centuries of our era. Essence is what is common to all, while person is the concrete entity that includes the essence. An illustration is in order: humanity is one but there are many human beings. Thus God is one but in three persons. Even though all three have and are of the same essence, each one has its own distinct attributes and functions. God is the source of the procession of both Son and Holy Spirit, and for that reason he is called Father; the Son is the Redeemer, the Person who became incarnate; the Holy Spirit is the Sanctifier, the person who perpetuates the redemptive work of the Son and proceeds from the Father.

Intellectual efforts have been made to explain the Trinity, but the Orthodox accept it as a mystery beyond the comprehension of the human mind.

When Orthodox Christians state in their creed that they "believe in one God, Father Almighty," they are speaking of God as a personal God, a God who speaks as I, who may be addressed as Thou or as Father, a God with personal attributes, with an insight, a concern, a plan for the destiny of the creation.

There are reasons that make faith of this type difficult. Watching the crowds on Broadway in New York City, standing under a starry sky and pondering the vastness and variety of nature, considering the wars among nations, one wonders whether a personal God is possible. There is among many modern intellectuals a disposition to view the universe as a machine, without feelings or soul, that ignores man's dreams, aspirations, and anxieties. People in the twentieth century have lost the sense of God as father, in the belief that to accept God in personal terms is unscientific or anachronistic.

There is justification for revolt against belief in a personal God, if God is presented in crude sensory terms. If the notion of God is that He is anthropomorphic, that He is an image of a man perhaps enormously large or a kind of Santa Claus, then there is much reason for intelligent people to reject belief in a personal God. However, to think of God in such physical terms is heresy, because "God is spirit, and those who worship him must worship in spirit and in truth" (Jn. 4:24).

The archaic Greeks thought of their gods on Olympos as eating, drinking, quarreling, loving, and procreating. But there was another kind of anthropomorphism, which did not debar them from thinking of God as personal. Anaxagoras, Socrates, and Plato denounced the beliefs of the earliest Greeks about the attributes of the divinity as blasphemy. They attributed to God other human qualities, such as thought, purpose, consciousness, personality. Ancient Greek religion went through stages of development as other religions did, including Judaism.

In the early part of the Old Testament there is a primitive anthropomorphism: God walks in the garden and calls for Adam and Eve, shuts the door of the ark, wrestles with Jacob, and so on. Later on, however, men like Amos and Hosea, Isaiah and Jeremiah, described the highest and holiest qualities of the second type of anthropomorphism. They attributed to God righteousness, justice, mercy, and fatherly love. The noblest qualities in man, they said, are but reflections of the attributes of God. In this sense, to say that God is personal, that He is Father Almighty, is to take what is finest and noblest in human consciousness and affirm its perfect existence in God.

When Jesus taught His disciples how to pray He began with the address "Our Father who art in heaven." "Father" means that God is not a cosmic principle, a diffuse or abstract being, but a living person, with authority, goodness, and love. Jesus Christ gave this term a centrality that transformed Western man's thoughts of God: God is Father because He brought man to spiritual life. Man is not to suffer from the fear of a terrible God, but to enjoy the love and affection of a fatherly God. In Orthodox theology God is *Philanthropos Theos*, that is, lover of human beings or a loving father.

Christianity asserts that through Christ man comes to understand and to feel the fatherhood of God. "But to all who received him, who believed in his name, he gave power to become children of God" (Jn. 1:12). Saint John writes elsewhere: "See what love the Father has given us, that we should be called children of God; and so we are" (1 Jn. 3:1). Since "no one has ever seen God; the only Son, who is in the bosom of the Father, he has made him known" (Jn. 1:18), Orthodox theology stresses that only by faith and spiritual experience can one confirm that God is Father. Religious experience is possible only if God is personal and if one maintains a personal relationship with him. God is both a being, personal, distinct from nature and man, and the being in whom all other beings participate and have their existence as distinct beings. People sense God in their own existence and come to know him fully through their interaction with themselves and other beings. The ancient Greek poet Aratos said: "In him we live and move and have our being" (Acts 17:28). But the Orthodox prefer to speak of what they do not know about the transcendence of God rather than of what logic and deduction can make of God. God is the "Great Mystery," but a mystery revealed in the life of Christ and in the life of every saint.

In the creed the Orthodox state that God is "Almighty, Maker of Heaven and Earth." God is *Pantokrator*, that is, "Almighty." The attribute "Almighty" needs no explanation, for if there is a God who made the heavens and the earth He certainly must be an almighty one. But why maker of heaven? What is heaven? Is heaven a place? "Heaven" is a term used to describe the atmosphere around our planet; the visible and the invisible material world; and the supernatural, or "metaphysical," spiritual world. All these aspects of heaven were made by God.

Is not such a teaching anachronistic? Has not science subverted the belief that God made everything? Has not the Bible, which is the source of this faith, been proven to be incompatible with science? These questions have been answered in the affirmative by clergymen and theologians who did not know science and by scientists who did not know the Bible.

The greatest disservice to the Christian faith has been done by theologians who tried to become scientists and by scientists who thought themselves theologians. The notion, held by both theologians and scientists, that the Bible can answer scientific questions has done incalculable harm and has caused immense confusion in the relations between science and religion. Several Greek Orthodox scientists in Greece have addressed themselves to these questions. In their journal, *Aktines*, they have complained about both theologians and clergymen whose teachings have been proven scientifically wrong. There is much misunderstanding about the teaching of the Bible and consequently about the doctrines of the Church, by theologians as well as scientists.

What does the Bible teach about the creation of the world? Does science contradict the Bible in this sphere of faith and knowledge? The Bible is not a textbook of science. The strength of the Bible lies in the fact that its function is not to impart scientific information, but to reveal God to man and to set forth a progressive spiritual revelation of the divine creator, culminating in the incarnation of Jesus Christ, God's Son and man's brother.

What basically are the teachings of the Holy Scriptures respecting the universe? The universe, with its harmony and order and rationality and all the bursting life that crowds the earth, came into existence through the creative activity of Almighty God. This teaching has nothing to do with the manner, that is, with the "how" of creation. The Bible writes about the "who," who is the author of creation. The "how" of creation is the prerogative of science. Faith answers the questions Whence? Where? Why? These constitute faith's inquiry. If this is the case, the question follows whether the Orthodox Church believes in evolution. The answer is that evolution is not necessarily antagonistic to faith. Saint Basil the Great implies a process of evolution in the creation of the world. The world was not created in time but with time. It is not necessary to believe that God made man as he is today but rather that He created the universe and man, which are the handiwork or overflowing of the inner attributes of God. God created all things "in heaven and on earth, visible and invisible . . .— all things were created through him and for him. He is before all things, and in him all things hold together," to use the language of Saint Paul (Col. 1:16–17).

Does science accept such an interpretation? Several leading scientists affirm that by using the scientific method of observation and experimentation they have arrived at the same conclusion as the writers and prophets of the Old and New Testaments who have recorded the august presence of God in the creation. Several Greek Orthodox scientists, such as Stavros Plakides and Demetrios Kotsakis, have written important books in defense of the Biblical account. Non-Orthodox scientists have expressed similar views.

Sir Oliver Lodge, the eminent physicist, writes:

> Science does not deal with origins—not ultimate origins. It takes the universe as a going concern and tries to explore it. In the beginning, and certainly there was a beginning to the solar system and the universe—there was the brooding of a divine spirit, an infinite Mind at work, planning and executing.

Another great scientist, Robert A. Millikan, winner of a Nobel prize for his achievement in isolating the electron, asserts that "there is not a shred of evidence that science has ever undermined a basic religious truth. Science and religion are sister forces working together for the advancement and the uplift of mankind." The spirit of religion and the spirit of science or knowledge are the two great pillars upon which all human well-being and human progress rest. It was on this basis perhaps that Albert Einstein wrote that "religion without science is lame, but science without religion is blind."

The Christ of the Orthodox

The second article of the creed reads: "[I believe] in one Lord Jesus Christ, the only begotten son of God . . . begotten not made, consubstantial with the Father, through whom all things were made." Greek Orthodox Christology constitutes a major segment of theology, which cannot be treated here extensively.

Six articles out of the twelve in the Nicene Creed deal with faith in Jesus Christ. This is very significant. While the majority of Christians believe in one God as proclaimed in the first article, many of them do not believe in Christ. This has been the problem from the very beginning of the history of Christianity: To convince people that Jesus Christ is what the creed proclaims Him to be. In the course of seven centuries the Christian Church was obliged to clarify her belief in Christ. As a result of this need, out of 174 words of the original Greek text of the creed, 109 deal with the person of Christ.

Christ was born some two thousand years ago, of a young woman not "married," in an out-of-the-way place called Bethlehem. We derive this information from several witnesses who were contemporaries of Christ's. Two of them were disciples of Christ, and one was a physician. Others also speak about the historicity of Jesus: the Jewish historian Josephus, the Roman biographer Suetonius, the Roman historians Tacitus and Pliny. There is no doubt whatsoever that Christ was born as a human being.

The historical records known as Gospels assert that Jesus grew up in an insignificant village named Nazareth. He belonged to a humble people, and to a low social class; He was denied the basic education of His day and people (Jn. 7:15); He was trained as a carpenter and lived an obscure life. At about thirty years of age He began to teach and preach and heal. "He went about doing good" (Acts 10:38). His whole life was lived in one troublesome province of the Roman Empire, and His travels were limited to an area half the size of Massachusetts. After three years of ministry, He was arrested on suspicion of leading a popular revolt and was executed by crucifixion.

Today nearly a third of mankind worships Him. Perhaps another third holds him in enormous respect. He has inspired beautiful music and great art in the Western world. People have died for Him in every generation. Many would die for Him even today. Some, even non-Christians such as Gandhi, consider that Christ's "new commandment" of love is the best law that can govern men.

Was this not a strange and unique person? Is it possible that everything concerning Christ might be a myth? It doesn't seem so. One eyewitness writes: "That which was from the beginning, which we have heard, which we have seen with our eyes, which we have looked upon and touched with our hands, . . . that which we have seen and heard we proclaim also to you" (1 Jn. 1:1, 3).

As a man Jesus suffered with those who suffered. He felt a profound sympathy for the people, who went about without purpose and leadership; He loved children and the poor; He had compassion for the sick, the blind, the afflicted, and the lonely; He was against fanaticism and spiritual hypocrisy; He forgave prostitutes and proclaimed justice, forgiveness, and love. He made some daring and unique claims for himself. "I am the way, and the truth, and the life," He said (Jn. 14:6); "the Son of man has authority on earth to forgive sins," He added (Lk. 5:24). One day He challenged His accusers, "Which of you convicts me of sin?" (Jn. 8:46).

The Christian Ecclesia, or community, was built on a conviction that He was God himself, "the . . . son of God, begotten of the Father before all ages" as the Nicene Creed states. Christians believe that there is one great God over all, but that in the oneness of God there are united three persons: the Father, the Son, and the Holy Spirit.

Christ as God the Son visibly appeared on earth, assuming human flesh, and was recorded in history. This man Jesus, who was also the Son of God, was God himself, who took upon himself humanity to disclose deity to man, who revealed the life of God to man that man might be able to reach out for God. So Jesus was both perfect man and perfect God, of eternal origin and existence, as the synod of Chalcedon (451) declared. In His person the expectations of the ancient world, of both Jews and Greeks, were fulfilled.

Matthew, the first important biographer of Jesus, writes that the Jewish Messianic expectations were fulfilled in Jesus. In the opening chapter of his record, Matthew gives a genealogy to prove that Christ is the Messiah of the Old Testament and descended from Abraham, David, and the kings of Judah. This lineage culminates in the birth of Christ, the expected Messiah.

Matthew's genealogy is arranged in three sections, which are based on three great stages in Jewish history. The first section takes the story of the Jews up to King David, who organized Israel into a strong kingdom. The second section takes the story through to the exile in Babylon, the period that includes the nation's humiliation and tragedy, and its expectation of a liberator, a Messiah. The third section takes the story up to Jesus Christ, the person who would free not only Israel but all mankind from its plight. Matthew's genealogy points out that ancient history culminates in the person of Christ, the alpha and omega, the beginning and end of Jewish history.

These three sections in Matthew's genealogy stand for three stages in the spiritual odyssey of Western man—if not in the history of mankind.

Man was made for eternity. "God created man in his own image, in the image of God he created him" (Gen. 1:27). God said: "Let us make man in our image, after our likeness" (Gen. 1:26). Man's spiritual attributes are divine attributes. Man was designed for eternal life in God. Not only the Old Testament but classical authors of antiquity spoke in this vein. Man was essentially born to be a little god, since his spirit is the spirit of God. Somehow man went astray and got lost.

Man's rebellion and disobedience to his creator is what the Orthodox call original sin. Instead of being the child of God, he became the slave of his own disobedience and folly and used his free will to defy God rather than to enter into friendship and *koinonia*, or fellowship, with his creator.

The third stage in the spiritual odyssey of mankind is redemption. In his fall, man was not abandoned. Into this world God sent the Messiah, the Christ, that He might rescue His children.

Christ is *Emmanuel* in Hebrew, which means "God with us" (Mt. 1:23). Emmanuel assumed human flesh in order to recreate man. Christ the Messiah was the fulfillment of the prophets' hopes and expectations.

In his genealogy Matthew shows the nobility of Jesus' earthly descent and stresses that he was the Messiah who would lead Israel to freedom and to ultimate salvation. The ancient Israelites were expectant people. Although their history was one long series of trials, although at the time of Jesus' birth the Jews were a subject people, they never forgot the promise that a messiah would liberate them. The ancient Greek and Roman pagans were also expectant people. Franz Cumont, a leading historian of Greco-Roman religious antiquity, sums up their expectations as follows: "The religious and mystical spirit of the Greco-Roman Orient . . . had prepared all nations to unite in the bosom of the universal Church of Christ." All nations were in need of a redeemer, all were dreaming of a messiah. The Jewish prophets wrote about the Messiah; the Greeks spoke about the Logos.

While for Matthew the Messianic expectations of ancient Israel were fulfilled in the person of Jesus Christ, the essence of the expectations of the Greeks was recorded by the author of Saint John's Gospel, who writes of the incarnation of the Logos. In the beginning of this brilliant Gospel, we read, "In the beginning was the Word [*Logos*], and the Word was with God, and the Word was God. He was in the beginning with God; all things were made through him, and without him was not anything made that was made" (Jn. 1:1–3).

When the author of the fourth Gospel writes of the Logos, or the Word, he means Jesus Christ. The writer had a definite purpose in mind when he called Jesus Christ the Logos, or the Word of God: To reconcile Greek thought with Christian faith.

The Christian Ecclesia was confronted from the start with a very basic problem. The Church had begun in Judaism. In the beginning all her members had been Jews or Hellenized Jews. By human descent Christ was a Jew, and except for brief visits to the districts of Tyre and Sidon and to the Hellenistic Decapolis, Jesus had never traveled in the Greek world. But although Christianity was cradled in Judaism, it very soon moved out into the wider world. Within thirty years of Jesus' death, by 60 A.D., Christianity had traveled all over Asia Minor and Greece proper and had arrived in Rome.

By that time there must have been thousands of Greeks in the Church. Jewish ideas were not well known to them. For example, the very center of Jewish expectations, the coming of the Messiah, was an idea quite alien to the Greeks. The very category in which the Jewish Christians conceived and spoke of Jesus meant nothing to a Greek. The problem thus became how to present Christianity to the Greek and Hellenized peoples. It has been observed that "the progress and spread of any idea depends, not only on the strength and force of the idea, but on the predisposition to receive it and on the age to which it is presented." Thus the task of the Christian Ecclesia was to create among the Greeks a predisposition to receive the Christian message. A Greek who was interested in Christianity should not be led through Jewish Messianic ideas and ways of thinking. The problem was to present Christ in such a way that anyone under the influence of Greek thought could understand and accept Him.

It seems that when John wrote his Gospel he was in the Greek city of Ephesos and was preoccupied with that problem. He sought to find a way to present Christianity to these Greeks in their own thought and in their own language, and he found the solution to the problem in the concept of the Logos. This concept existed in both Greek and late Jewish thought, and was something that both could understand.

As we have said, the Jews for more than three hundred and fifty years before Christ had been exposed to Greek culture. With the conquest of Palestine by Alexander the Great and the dissemination of Greek thought and Greek influence, the concept of the Logos of God was assimilated into Hebrew religious thought. For more than a hundred years before the coming of Christ, Hebrew was a forgotten language among the Jews in Alexandria and in other cities of the Hellenic world. The Old Testament, originally written in Hebrew, was translated into Greek for the Jews who no longer knew Hebrew—the translation known as the Septuagint. In this transitional period the name of God came to be known by the Jews as the "Word of God," or the "Reason of God," both "Word" and "Reason" translating the Greek *Logos*.

The Jewish concept of the Logos was developed much further in the so-called Wisdom Literature, Proverbs and Wisdom of Solomon, which were written about the year 100 B.C. In these two books the Word, the Logos of God, and His wisdom appear as the instruments of creation. The Logos makes the will of God known to the mind and heart of man. It was Philo, the Hellenized Jew, who further developed this concept under the influence of Greek thought. Philo tried to reconcile Old Testament faith with Greek philosophical thought and became a link between the two worlds.

The idea of the Logos fit into Greek thought perfectly. It had appeared about 560 B.C., whether providentially or accidentally, in Ephesos, where the fourth Gospel was to be written. The Logos theory was enunciated by the Greek philosopher Heraklitos, whose basic idea was that everything in this world is in a state of flux. His famous illustration was that "it is impossible to step twice into the same river."

Despite the fact that everything is in constant flux, life is not chaos because it is controlled and ordered; it is systematically following a continuous pattern; and that which controls the pattern is the Logos, the *Nous* (or Mind), the Word, the Reason of God. To Heraklitos, to Plato, to the Stoic philosophers, and to other Greek thinkers, the Logos was the principle of order under which the universe continued to exist.

According to Greek thought the Logos was the creating and directing power of God, the power that made the universe and preserves it. As Matthew used Hebrew theology, so John used Greek theology, and spoke in categories familiar to the Greeks. To use William Barclay's paraphrase:

> For centuries you have been thinking and writing, and dreaming about the Logos, the power which keeps the order in the Universe, the power by which men think and reason and know, the power by which men come into contact with God. This Logos became flesh. Jesus Christ is that Logos. In Christ is perfectly revealed to men all that God always was and always will be, and all that God feels towards and desires for men.

Not only John but Paul and other New Testament authors used Greek thought and terms in order to make Christianity acceptable to the Greeks.

The Orthodox believe that Christ, whether Messiah or Logos, was born by the Holy Spirit and of the Virgin Mary to be the agent of the regeneration and salvation of man. The Orthodox believe in the miraculous appearance of God among men; they subscribe to the virgin birth of Christ as stated in the Nicene Creed.

Belief in the way Christ was born has been controversial in the history of Christianity. There are Christians who find it hard to believe that Christ was born of a virgin, even though it is an article of faith in the Nicene Creed. The Orthodox doctrine on the virgin birth rests both on the Bible and on logic. The Bible states: "That which is conceived in her [Mary] is of the Holy Spirit" (Mt. 1:20). This statement is based on the prophecy of Isaiah, who wrote: "Behold, a virgin shall conceive in the womb, and shall bring forth a son and you shall call his name Emmanuel" (Is. 7:14), a name which means "God with us" (Mt. 1:23). But the virgin birth should be examined in the context of the totality of Jesus' life. If Christ was the Son of God, the Logos who became flesh, who lived an unusual and sinless life, who taught extraordinary things, who died an unusual death and rose from the dead, it is not difficult to accept the virgin birth. If Christ was a person apart, lived differently from all others, made unique claims for himself, and had an unparalleled impact on history, it is not difficult to accept that His entrance into human life was as unusual as His leaving it.

Pascal, the French philosopher, once remarked: "Why cannot a virgin bear a child? Does a hen not lay eggs without a cock? What distinguishes these eggs outwardly from others? And who has told us that the hen may not form the germ as well as the cock?" Which carried the·germ of life, the egg of the mother or the sperm of the father? What or who is the source of life? Such questions and others like them, which refer to the mystery of life, prompted Dr. Elias Gyftopoulos, a distinguished professor at the Massachusetts Institute of Technology, to tell me some time ago: "Every time I speak with a biologist or a biochemist my admiration for the mystery of creation deepens and my wonder increases."

If one accepts Jesus Christ as God, the incarnate Messiah of the Jews and the Logos of the Greeks, there is no difficulty in also accepting His supernatural appearance among men. God selected the same method to re-create mankind that He had used to create mankind. As God had created man by direct intervention, so He elected to re-create mankind in a similar manner. Saint Irenaios, one of the early Church Fathers, writes that as "the first man Adam had no human father and he was the direct creation of God, likewise the New Adam, [i.e. Jesus Christ,] who was to re-create man, was the straightforward work of God, the Holy Spirit."

In the Scriptures the Spirit of God is closely associated with the work of creation. It was through the Spirit that God created. In the beginning the Spirit of God moved upon the face of the waters, and the chaos evolved into a beautiful universe. Likewise the Spirit is associated with the work of re-creation. In the birth of Christ, the new Adam, the being who re-created mankind, the Spirit of God was operative as never before. It was the Spirit who was God's agent in the creation of the universe and it was the Spirit who alone could re-create fallen mankind. Thus it was by the Holy Spirit that the Virgin Mary conceived Jesus.

But the Orthodox believe that Christ "for us men and for our salvation came down from heaven and was incarnate . . . ." This statement first proclaims the *reason* for the coming of the Son of God upon the earth; second, it speaks about the *incarnation* itself; and third, it tells about the *manner* of the incarnation.

Throughout the Bible man is told that "Christ Jesus came into the world to save sinners" (1 Tim. 1:15). Christ Himself said: "I came not to call the righteous, but sinners." (Mt. 9:13). "The Son of man came to seek and to save the lost," He proclaims elsewhere (Lk. 19:10). "Our sin caused the manifestation of the philanthropy of God in the person of Jesus Christ," asserts Saint Athanasios. The fall of man from the grace of God occasioned the incarnation of His Son and His ministry among men.

Man was deprived of God's fellowship by his disobedience, and God took the initiative in restoring it. Christ is the *theanthropos,* or the God-Man. In the course of the centuries, and following a great deal of searching theological discussion, the Church laid down in two great councils (the fourth and the sixth general, or ecumenical synods) a doctrine that in Christ, the Messiah-Logos, there is one person "in two natures [which exist] without confusion, without change, without division, without separation." There was no other way for man to be saved except through the God-made-man event, or the humanization of the deity. Orthodox anthropology and Christology have lost little of their original formulations. Thus modern Orthodox theology believes that modern man is lost in confusion and uncertainty, notwithstanding his scientific and technological achievements, his progress in medicine, economy, and other areas of human endeavor. He has been invited to appropriate the attributes of the God-man, Christ, so that he may be transformed into the Christ icon, or image. The humanized deity is here to deify the human. Man without the divine in himself is not certain of his destiny. He is in need of divine guidance. Paul summarized the human situation very poignantly in his letter to the Romans: "I can will what is right, but I cannot do it. For I do not do the good I want, but the evil I do not want is what I do. Now if I do what I do not want, it is no longer I that do it, but sin which dwells within me" (Rom. 7:18–20).

Sinful nature controls humankind, which wants peace in the world but prepares for war; which needs more ploughs but makes more guns; which wants a cure for cancer but spends most of its wealth making bigger and "better" bombs. Medicine confirms that smoking causes cancer but man goes on making "better" cigarettes and more elaborate commercials for tobacco. There is an element within human beings that leads them to self-destruction.

Man's fall from communion with God has caused a dichotomy in man. He combines the will of God with desire for evil: beauty and ugliness, kindness and cruelty, peace and warlike qualities, are in every man. The angelic and the demonic are in constant conflict. It was man's need to regain his pristine purity and his original association with his Creator-Father that prompted the incarnation of Christ. Christ is called Savior, because His main purpose in coming to this earth was to save people from their schizophrenic condition, from this cacophony of human nature, to save them from sin and redeem them for eternity. But Christ was rejected, crucified, and buried.

That Christ was crucified in time and in space has been confirmed by history. Death by crucifixion was called by Cicero "the most cruel and the most horrible torture." Tacitus called it "a torture fit only for slaves." Was the crucifixion necessary? Why did Jesus allow himself to be crucified? This was His purpose, "To reconcile the two [Jews and Gentiles] in a single body to God through the cross, on which he killed the enmity" (Eph. 2:16).

Orthodox Christians greatly honor the cross of Christ, which is a sacred symbol in their spiritual life. The crucifixion manifests how loving God is. The cross symbolizes the supreme power of God to transform defeat into triumph through sacrificial love.

Jesus said· "If any man would come after me, let him deny himself and take up his cross and follow me" (Mk. 8:34). The Orthodox find in this passage the center of their Christian faith and an explanation of their historical vicissitudes. The Orthodox observe three great holy days that remind them of the cross—Holy Friday, the Exaltation of the Cross, and the Third Sunday of Lent.

However, the cross is not the final word in Orthodox theology. In fact, the resurrection of Christ is the focal point of Orthodox theology and worship. Easter is the most theologically significant holy day in Greek Christianity, because the resurrection is the foundation stone of early Christianity. The Orthodox believe that, as a religion, Christianity stands or falls with belief in the resurrection. The very existence of the Christian Ecclesia is based on the proclamation of the risen Christ. How was it possible for certain Galilean fishermen to establish the Church without some amazing event as a background? The resurrection was announced three days after Jesus' death, and it was publicly and effectively preached within eight weeks. Matthew, Mark, Luke, John, Paul, and Peter, who wrote about the resurrection, are historical figures, and their testimony has withstood careful and critical examination in the course of twenty centuries. The Orthodox dismiss theories that try to explain the resurrection rationally—such as that Christ was not dead when they took Him from the cross and that His friends removed him from the sepulcher, which would imply that Jesus' disciples spent the rest of their lives preaching a lie they were prepared to die for.

What is the answer to the claim that the resurrection was a hallucination? Hallucination usually takes place in a climate of expectation, and the disciples were not expecting the resurrection. Thomas was as uncompromising as a man could be. He would not believe when his ten friends tried to assure him that it was true. The disciples as yet "did not know the scripture, that he must rise from the dead" (Jn. 20:9). John, Peter, Thomas, Mary Magdalene, Mary the mother of James, and Salome saw the risen Christ. Hallucination can account for some paradoxical things, but not for the event that became the cornerstone of the early Christians' faith.

The historicity of the cross and resurrection has sustained itself for almost two thousand years. It is true that it has been a stumbling block throughout the history of Christianity—"a stumbling block to Jews and folly to Gentiles," (1 Cor. 1:23), for the "Jews demand signs and Greeks seek wisdom" (1 Cor. 1:22). Nevertheless, as Paul writes, for believers, both Jews and Greeks, the risen Christ revealed the power and wisdom of God (1 Cor. 1:24).

These are the grounds, then, upon which the Orthodox stand and observe Easter not only for forty days but every Sunday of the year, for every Sunday serves as a reminder of the resurrection. In the Orthodox world the Easter season is preeminently the festival of triumph and of hope, the victory over death, the festival of life, and the confirmation of eternal life after death.

Life after death is an extremely important article of the Orthodox creed. Not a few biologists and other scientists assert that there is no life after death. These same biologists may admit, however, that one can never know what life is. But if they do not know what life is, how can they be so certain that there is no life after death? Science cannot give a satisfactory answer, for the time being at least, as to what life is and whether there is life after death. Christianity, which believes that life is the spirit, the power, the energy, and the manifestation of God, is certain about life after death: Christ said: "I am the resurrection and the life; he that believes in me, though he were dead, yet shall he live: and whosoever lives and believes in me shall never die" (Jn 11:25–26). Death is another state of being, in which the spirit has returned to God and continues to live in God, who created it.

Christianity is not alone in its faith in life after death. Non-Christian intellectuals and spiritual people of all times have also believed in it from antiquity to modern times. The Church approaches life and death by faith, as people approach by faith the automobile, the airplane, the physician, the dentist, or the pharmacist. People believe because there are things they cannot explain. The immortality of the human being is in perfect agreement with human nature. God the architect, who created as wonderful a creature as the human person, would not destroy it after lavishing so much care on it. All the events of the crucifixion, the burial, and Easter point to life and eternity.

The Holy Spirit

The opening prayer in the Orthodox prayer book is directed to the Holy Spirit, who is described as the "Paraclete" and the "Spirit of Truth," while the creed speaks of "the Giver of Life." What is the Holy Spirit? He is the third person of the Holy Trinity, one person of the same essence with the other two persons of the one Christian God.

The Orthodox Church has been characterized as a pneumatological church, because she lays such great emphasis upon the work of the Holy Spirit. She describes the whole purpose of the Christian life on earth as the acquisition of the Holy Spirit. A saint has put it in the following terms: "Prayer, fasting, vigils, and all other Christian practices, however good they may be in themselves, certainly do not constitute the aim of our Christian life: they are but the indispensable means of attaining that aim. For the true aim of the Christian life is the acquisition of the Holy Spirit of God." Fasts, vigils, prayers, charities, and other good works done in the name of Christ are the means of acquiring the Holy Spirit of God. The prayer life of the faithful starts with the invocation of the Holy Spirit. Every morning the Orthodox place themselves under the protection of the Holy Spirit when they recite the beautiful prayer: "O Heavenly King, O comforter, the Spirit of truth, who art everywhere and fillest all things, the treasury of blessings and giver of life, come and abide in us. Cleanse us from all impurity, and of your goodness save our souls."

But why so much emphasis on the Holy Spirit? Because the Holy Spirit is the Spirit of God, the life-giving power of God, the promulgator of Christ's work in the salvation and eternal destiny of man. Jesus Christ promised His apostles that "the Holy Spirit, whom the Father will send in my name, he will teach you all things, and bring to your remembrance all that I have said to you" (Jn. 14:26).

The Holy Spirit continues the work of Jesus through inspired human beings. He carries on the redemption and sanctification of man. He reveals and preaches the good tidings through people, through prophets, the Fathers, and the saints of the Church. The Holy Spirit speaks to man's heart and transforms him into a new creation, through repentance and Christ's teachings.

The Holy Spirit's power leads the human person to achieve the final aim of the Christian life, the *theosis*, or deification, of human nature, a notion very dear to the Orthodox. *Theosis* means life in God, the transformation of a human being into a little god within God. This notion is in perfect agreement with the Scriptures. Once people picked up stones to cast at Christ. When Jesus asked why they were doing this, the people answered that it was because He was insulting God by calling himself God. And Jesus answered: "Is it not written in your law, 'I said, you are gods'?" (Jn. 10:34; Ps. 82:6). Thus Jesus himself calls man a little god. This teaching has been taken over by the Fathers and the tradition of the Church. It constitutes an important element of the eschatological teachings of the Greek Orthodox Church.

Saint Basil the Great describes man as a creature who has received the order to become a god; and Saint Athanasios, as is well known, has expressed it in the classic words "God became man that man might become God." And the Church, in the hymn for Holy Thursday matins, sings as follows: "In my kingdom, said Christ, I shall be God with you as Gods" (cf. Ps. 82:6; Jn. 10:34).

The great theological quests of the fourth and the fifth centuries ultimately resulted in the affirmation that salvation is the divinization of humanity and its absorption in God, the source of its life. Damnation is exactly the opposite, the deprivation of God's presence in the life of humanity. The deification of the human has its beginnings here on earth, but it will reach its fulfillment in the life to come. It is the result of man's response to the presence of the Holy Spirit in man's life.

The Holy Spirit works in human beings through the sacraments of the Church and through reading and listening to the Holy Scriptures. Christ promised that the Holy Spirit would teach the Church all things necessary for man's salvation. To the end of time the Holy Spirit will be leading the faithful and the Church into deeper and deeper understanding of the truth of God.

The Holy Spirit guides the Church, or the community, in understanding the meaning of Jesus' teachings, which would not otherwise be possible. Upon the departure of Christ from the earth, the Holy Spirit came to inspire, guide, and establish the Ecclesia and to remain with it forever. "I will not leave you desolate," Jesus promised His disciples (Jn. 14:18). In this respect Jesus proved different from other great teachers. Plato writes that, when Socrates died, his disciples "thought that [they] would have to spend the rest of their lives orphans, as children bereft of a father, and [they] did not know what to do about it." The Paraclete took Jesus' place and remains forever with the disciples. It is the Spirit, then, who gives purpose in life and who remains with the Church forever as "the Lord, the Giver of Life."

The Church

The Orthodox belief in "One holy, catholic and apostolic Church," as stated in the Nicene Creed, is of great significance.

A great deal of what separates Christians today depends on their concept of what the Church is. For the Orthodox, the Church is the community of people that believes in the living God, as revealed by Christ, and that is governed by the Holy Spirit. This spiritual institution is God's creation for man's salvation. It is an organism rather than an organization for social, political, or charitable purposes, though these, too, are important functions of the Church. The Church is the Ecclesia, the gathering, or union, of people who are bound together by the same faith, style of life, and worship. It is a community of God and people, in which a person is purified, reformed, and immortalized through one baptism and continuous communion with God.

Despite the wide disagreement among Christians as to the exact nature of the Church, all agree that the Ecclesia was established by the Holy Spirit through the Apostles to be the true promulgator of the work of Christ. The Ecclesia has been set apart in holiness as a worshipping community, a community whose leading constituents are Christ and the Holy Spirit.

Saint Paul describes the Church as *oikon Theou . . . stylon kai ethreoma tes aletheias*. That is, it is the household of God and the pillar and foundation of truth (1 Tim. 3:15). Paul implies that the Church is first and foremost a family of believers, where the love of God and brotherly love prevail. Christians belonging to the Church possess true feelings of togetherness, of close family relationship. It is for this reason that the Greek Orthodox feel such an intimate relationship with the Church, which has so well served their religious as well as other spiritual and social needs.

The Church, furthermore, is an assembly, an organization, in its sociological character. The term *ekklesia* literally means a company of people who have been called out (from the Greek *ek kalo*). It does not mean that they have been selected. In ancient Athens the *ekklesia tou demou* was the governing body of the city; and the governing body consisted of all the citizens met in assembly. All the citizens were summoned to the assembly, but not all attended. In a similar way, the religious use of the term *ekklesia* implies that God's invitation has gone out to every man, but only some have responded. Those who have accepted it are the assembly—the Ekklesia.

Saint Paul describes the Church as the pillar of truth. He wrote about the Church in this manner to Timothy, giving instructions for the Christians of Ephesos. In Ephesos the term *pillar* had a special significance. The greatest monument in Ephesos was the temple of Artemis (Diana). "Great is Artemis of the Ephesians!" (Acts 19:28). That temple was one of the seven wonders of antiquity and among its features were its pillars—one hundred and twenty-seven of them. All were made of marble, and some were adorned with jewels and overlaid with gold. The Christians of Ephesos understood well how beautiful a pillar could be. The symbol here is of the duty of the Ecclesia to hold up the truth in such a way that all people can see it. It is the duty of the Church not only to baptize, marry, and bury people, but to demonstrate the truth. The Church as an organization is concerned with social functions and social issues, but as the organism of God and His people her primary function is to lead people to God's bosom. Furthermore, the Ecclesia is described by Saint Paul as the foundation of truth. The truth is identified with the Christian faith. It is the function of the Church to protect and maintain it.

The Greek Orthodox Church possesses certain attributes that deserve to be briefly analyzed. The church is Orthodox, for it embodies and proclaims the *orthe doxa,* that is, the right faith in Christ. What Christ taught and His disciples interpreted is still so taught and so interpreted. There is harmony in all essentials between the present Church and the original Church, a harmony that secures tranquility and internal balance, thereby preserving the faith from extremes. The regulator of this harmony and continuity is the Holy Spirit, who abides with the Church and guides the Church to all the truth necessary to salvation (Mt. 28:20; Jn. 14:26).

The term "Orthodox" was used by the early Church to distinguish the true faithful from heretics and followers of false teachings. Saint Paul speaks indirectly of it when he asserts that after his time, "some shall depart from the faith, giving heed to seducing spirits and doctrines of devils" (1 Tim. 4:1). The

Lord warns that there are heretics and false prophets who come among men "in sheep's clothing" (Mt. 7:15). The Bible speaks of Orthodoxy when it teaches against "false prophets" and "false teachers . . . who secretly shall bring in damnable heresies" (2 Pet. 2:1; cf. 1 Cor. 11:19, Tit. 3:10, Gal. 5:20). The word "Orthodox" does not simply mean the true teaching about God: It also suggests the true faith, the true life, the true worship on the part of the believer. Thus, *orthe doxa* also implies *orthe praxe,* right faith and right life. The historic Church pursued not only *orthodoxia* in faith, but *orthopraxia* in everyday life as well.

The Church is also Orthodox because she is the original Christian Church. In the twentieth century she remains the depository and true preserver of early Christian faith, culture, and life, which were universally accepted and attested to in the early centuries of our era. The present Church evidences an unbroken continuity that, by way of the ecumenical synods and the Church Fathers, reaches back to the apostolic Church and our Lord himself. Her Orthodoxy is not a static element that makes her a dormant body of creeds and traditions. It is rather a living attribute that receives its inspiration from the Holy Scriptures, the sacred tradition, and the Church Fathers; that is, it is the work of the Holy Spirit throughout the history of the Church. Orthodoxy, then, provides a continuous reinterpretation and vibrant communication of the revelation of God. She remains the mainstream of the Church of Pentecost, which flows slowly but steadily in the field of history.

The Church is Catholic in that her message of salvation in Christ is destined for the whole of mankind, for God "desires all men to be saved and to come to the knowledge of the truth" (1 Tim. 2:4) and Christ "gave himself as a ransom for all" (1 Tim. 2:6). The doors of the Church are open to all, with no discrimination as to race, nationality, or sex. "There is neither Jew nor Greek, there is neither slave nor free, there is neither male nor female" (Gal. 3:28). The Church is Catholic because she embraces the totality (the *kath olou*) of truth necessary for man's happiness and salvation. Being the body of Christ on earth, the Church is what her head claimed to be, "the way, and the truth" (Jn. 14:6). Christ himself promised that the Holy

Spirit would guide the Church "into all the truth" (Jn. 16:13). Jesus prayed that His Church might be sanctified in the truth (Jn. 17:17) and commanded his disciples to go and teach all nations (Mt. 28:19).

The last attribute of the Church is apostolicity. The Church was "built upon the foundation of the apostles . . . Christ Jesus himself being the cornerstone" (Eph. 2:20). She has retained the apostolic faith through the apostolic succession of her officers and through the tradition of the Church, which has maintained her unity with the ancient Church, a unity in spirit, in faith, and in truth.

Life in the Church

As we have indicated earlier, the Greek Orthodox Church has mysteries, or sacraments. The mysteries of the Church are rites and services through which special gifts are bestowed upon men. Though these mysteries transmit supernatural grace, they convey it to man by external and visible means. Like the Church herself, they include both supernatural and material elements. The theanthropic nature of Christ is extended both to His Church and to her means of grace. The Orthodox Church has not accepted any mysteries by formal decree. However, the following have been accepted as mysteries *de facto*.

REBIRTH AND ILLUMINATION

By means of this sacrament one crosses the threshold of the earthly Kingdom of God through forgiveness of sins, and becomes a member of the Church, of the body of Christ. "Be baptized . . . for the forgiveness of your sins" was the advice of Saint Peter (Acts 2:38; cf. Acts 22:16). Furthermore, baptism is a participation in the death, resurrection, and eternal life of Christ (Rom. 6:3–4). Infant baptism, which was introduced in the early Church, is still practiced. Together with the parents, the sponsor becomes responsible for the child's upbringing in the Christian Orthodox faith.

Though most Orthodox Christians today are born in the Orthodox Church, there are many who have joined it from other religious creeds. In recent years group conversions of Moslems and non-Orthodox Christians to the Orthodox faith have taken place in northern Greece, Uganda, and Tanzania. The Greek Church does not preach the gospel among people to whom Christ has been proclaimed, in accordance with Saint Paul's example: "To preach the gospel, not where Christ has already been named, lest I build on another man's foundation, but as it is written, 'They shall see who have never been told of him, and they shall understand who have never heard of him' " (Rom. 15:20–21). But there are many converts every year from various Christian denominations in such countries as Great Britain, France, Germany, and the United States. Outside the contiguous United States, the Greek Orthodox Church supports missionary activity in Alaska, Mexico, Uganda, and Korea. Today there is an ever-increasing zeal for missionary activity in non-Christian territories.

The Orthodox have condemned the practice of some Western Churches of sending missionaries, in centuries past and as late as the first half of the twentieth century, to such Christian countries as Greece and to other Christian communities in the Near East. Such missions have been responsible for conflicts and divisions among Christians and as a whole have failed in converting non-Christians. Several such American missions continue to create problems for Greek Orthodox jurisdictions. Thus in Greece in particular there is a great deal of complaint against American missionary activity. The Greek Orthodox consider Jesus' warning as appropriate: "Woe to you, . . . for you traverse sea and land to make a single proselyte, and when he becomes a proselyte, you make him twice as much a child of hell as yourselves." (Mt. 23:15).

Baptism is followed by the sacrament of Holy Chrism. It is administered immediately after baptism and corresponds to the laying on of hands or anointing with chrism of New Testament times. Through this sacrament the newly baptized receives the seal and the gifts of the Holy Spirit (Acts 2:38), and it constitutes the completion of baptism. It could be compared to confirmation, which is practiced in non-Orthodox Churches.

BREAD FROM HEAVEN

In addition to baptism and Chrism, the faithful need constant spiritual nourishment for the preservation and cultivation of their spiritual life. Thus, there is the sacrament of the Holy Eucharist. "He who eats my flesh and drinks my blood abides in me, and I in him" (Jn. 6:56, cf. Mt. 26:26). Since the Orthodox believe in the real presence of Jesus in the sacrament, the Eucharist occupies a very important place in the life of the Orthodox Christian. The Orthodox Catholic Church places this great emphasis on the Eucharist because of its faith in the Biblical account.

The Jews had received innumerable "signs" from God. God proved His faithfulness, His love, and His providence by various signs in Old Testament times. God planned and executed their liberation from Egypt. He gave them manna to eat and water to drink in the wilderness.

In New Testament times, the Jews demanded similar signs from Christ in order to believe and follow Him. "What sign are you going to perform that we may see it and believe in you?" they asked. "Our fathers ate the manna in the wilderness . . . He gave them bread from heaven to eat' " (Jn. 6:31). Saint Paul wrote: "Jews demand signs and Greeks seek wisdom" (1 Cor. 1:22).

Jesus offers himself, His very body and His very blood, as heavenly manna for the nourishment not only of ancient Israel but of the new one as well. Christ explains that the bread that ancient Israel had received was not eternal, it was not from heaven; it was something temporary, material, and perishing. But now He offers "the living bread which came down from heaven; if any one eats of this bread, he will live for ever" (Jn. 6:51). This bread of God is Jesus himself.

> I am the bread of life. Your fathers ate the manna in the wilderness, and they died. This is the bread which comes down from heaven, that a man may eat of it and not die. I am the living bread which came down from heaven; if any one eats of this bread, he will live forever; and the bread which I shall give for the life of the world is my flesh. . . . Truly, truly, I say to you, unless you eat the flesh of the Son of man and drink his blood, you have no life in you . . . For my flesh is food indeed, and my blood is drink indeed. He who eats my flesh and drinks my blood abides in me, and I in him (Jn. 6:48–56).

Jesus spoke these enigmatic words almost a year before His death. And a few days before His crucifixion, at the Last Supper, Jesus took a loaf of bread and blessed it; He broke it in pieces and gave it to His disciples, saying, " 'Take, eat, this is my body.' And he took a cup, and when he had given thanks he gave it to them, saying, 'Drink of it, all of you; for this is my blood of the covenant, which is poured out for many for the forgiveness of sins' " (Mt. 26:26–28).

By virtue of this evidence, the Eucharist is not only the center of Christian worship but also the very heart of the Christian way of life. The Eucharist of the Greek Orthodox Church is nothing less than the re-enactment of the life, the teaching, the death, and the resurrection of our Lord. It is a mystery by which the life and sacrifice of Christ are commemorated; it is the offering of His Life as the imperishable manna. Saint Paul states that he learned from Christ himself the significance of His Last Supper. He repeatedly indicates that Christians must perform this act of commemoration in remembrance of Jesus' sacrifice, of the Lord's death (1 Cor. 11:23–29).

The term "Eucharist" signifies "thanksgiving." Jesus offered himself as the supreme sacrifice to God the Father and commanded that this offering be reenacted in remembrance of himself. Thus, the Orthodox priest acts in Christ's stead when he performs the divine liturgy. "He reproduces what Christ did, and he then offers a true and complete sacrifice to God the Father" (Saint Cyprian).

As the observance of the Passover reminded ancient Israel of its liberation from Egypt, so the Eucharist reminds the Christian of the sacrifice of the Son of God. People write biographies, erect monuments of art, paint pictures, and record histories lest they forget. The divine Eucharist is celebrated as true sacrifice, as remembrance, as communion, and as thanksgiving.

There is abundant evidence that the Apostolic Church extensively celebrated the sacrament of the Eucharist. Saint Ignatios of Antioch advises the Christians of Ephesos "to meet frequently to celebrate God's Eucharist and to offer praise." It "is the medicine of immortality, the antidote to death, and everlasting life in Jesus Christ."

The Eucharist, therefore, is the new sign that God gave to

Christians. The faithful—the Christians—must celebrate the Eucharist as often as possible, to express thanks to God the Father for the great condescension of His Son. This mystery of the body and blood of Christ is a realization of the unity of all true believers with Christ and with all the members of his holy body—the Church. Through the sacrament of the Eucharist, human nature enters into union with the divine nature of Christ. Our humanity becomes consubstantial with the deified humanity of Christ, as Vladimir Lossky writes. Thereby, through Holy Communion, a corporeal unity of man with Christ is achieved. This is not a symbol like the sign for which the Jews asked Jesus, or a sign that would be foolishness to the Greeks, but a sign full of mystery and wisdom. It may perplex some people or appear as absurdity to others who demand reasons, but for Orthodox Christians it demonstrates their faith in God's power and wisdom (cf. 1 Cor. 1:24).

RENEWAL AND SPIRITUAL GROWTH

The Christian way of life is one of constant ascent and continuous effort toward spiritual growth and moral perfection. The faithful are reminded that their ultimate goal is to "become partakers of the divine nature" (2 Pet. 1:4) and to achieve *theosis*, perpetual life in God. Guided by this ideal, the Church admonishes her members to strive as Christ enjoined them: "Be perfect, as your heavenly Father is perfect" (Mt. 5:48). And Christ's Apostles taught that Christians "should be holy and blameless" (Eph. 1:4) and that "as he who called you is holy, be holy yourselves in all your conduct; since it is written, 'You shall be holy, for I am holy' " (1 Peter 1:15–16). The emphasis on spirituality and renewal has been a characteristic of monasticism. But how does one become "perfect" and "holy" in an imperfect and sinful world?

To be a baptized Christian is not a guarantee of instant salvation or of a sinless life. The Church has never claimed to be a museum of "holy" people or "saints." Instead, she has taught that the Church is a hospital for sinners who seek their spiritual health. Not only is the restoration to spiritual health of the greater sinner sought, but the improvement of those who are healthier is constantly encouraged. Orthodox spirituality views the believer's life as a ceaseless *gignesthai,* an unremitting becoming, never static or in a state in which perfection has been reached and salvation has been secured. Thus an Orthodox will never say, "I am saved," but always, "Through the grace and the help of God I hope to be saved." It is God who determines who is and who is not saved. Living in the world means daily confronting the sins and the imperfections of the world, which may influence believers and lead them away from God and His Church.

The best guard against allowing sin to become a permanent state of being, and the most effective way of restoring relations between man and God, is *metanoia,* repentance. The Greek word *metanoia* means change of mind and ways. Jesus began His ministry with a call to *metanoia,* and John the Baptist prepared the way for Christ's ministry with a call to repentance (Mt. 3:2, 4:17). John and Jesus called upon Israel to repent and return to the principles of the covenant that had been established between God and Israel. In a Christian context, *metanoia* means a change of mind and intellect, accompanied by contrition and regret for sins committed whether by deed, word, or thought. The world is viewed as potentially saved but not saved *per se.* The Church as a community of people is composed of repenting sinners being continually cleansed by the Holy Spirit through *metanoia.*

Basically *metanoia,* or repentance, is a spiritual crisis, an act of conversion, the result of an *autognosia,* a self-knowledge, when one comes to oneself. The criminal repents for his act of homicide or robbery; the angry person for his words of wrath and insult; and the devout and pious for an evil or improper thought. All are acts of repentance, though they differ in degree. As Saint Isaac Syrios put it: "Repentance is fitting at all times and for all persons. To sinners as well as to the righteous who look for salvation. There are no bounds to perfection, for even the perfection of the most perfect is nought but imperfection. Hence, until the moment of death neither the time nor the works of repentance can ever be complete." This understanding of renewal and spiritual growth recognizes the principle that "the more perfect one becomes, the more one is aware of one's own imperfections."

Regardless of how grave one's sins may be, the Church, as God's people and instrument, forgives and receives back the repentant, as the father in the parable received back his prodigal son when "he came to himself" and decided to return home. The Church teaches that a sinner should never despair—no matter how great the sin. The Church's attitude rests on "God's unfathomable *philanthropia*—love." As Saint John Chrysostom put it: "Do you sin every day? Do repent every day!" For "in the act of repentance God's *philanthropia* is outpoured, and there is no measure to count or estimate God's *philanthropia* and no word can explain God's immeasurable goodness."

The Church, however, expects not only an inner contrition and crisis but also an external acknowledgment of the inner crisis, and a confession before the Church's representative, either a bishop or a priest—the father confessor. The authority of the Church to accept repentance, forgive sins, and renew one's membership in the Church rests on the words of Christ, who charged His disciples with these words: "If you forgive the sins of any, they are forgiven; if you retain the sins of any, they are retained" (Jn. 20:23; cf. Mt. 18.18). Confession as a cleansing of the inner being serves as the renewal of baptism and corresponds to a psychological need. It unloads a heavy conscience and purifies mind and soul. "If we confess our sins, He [Christ] is faithful and just, and will forgive our sins and cleanse us from all unrighteousness," the Apostle writes (1 Jn. 1:9).

In the Orthodox Church, confession is practiced in a personal, fatherly manner between the penitent and the father confessor, who serves not only as the instrument of forgiveness and reassurance but also as a counsellor, adviser, spiritual guide. But, as in other Church sacraments, the father confessor is not the source but the instrument of forgiveness. He never says "I forgive you," because God alone is the source of forgiveness; instead he says, "You are forgiven through me, a sinner." The father confessor serves only as an earthen vessel conveying God's grace.

DIVINE POWER IN EARTHEN VESSELS

Life in the Church is served and guided by ordained people. Ordination is in agreement with the teaching of the Holy Scriptures and the experience of the early and medieval Church. The Bible indicates clearly that there is a distinction among the faithful of Christ, which in modern terms can be described as that between "clergy" and "laity." Saint Luke tells us that Jesus had many disciples from whom he chose only twelve: Jesus "went out into the hills to pray; and all night he continued in prayer to God. And when it was day, he called his disciples, and chose from them twelve, whom he named apostles" (Lk. 6:12–13).

Luke also states that the seven first deacons were elected by the faithful and ordained by the twelve Apostles. The seven candidates were "set before the apostles, and they laid their hands upon them" (Acts 6:6). Likewise, when Barnabas and Paul were sent out to evangelize, the prophets and teachers of the Christian community, after having fasted and prayed, "laid their hands on them" (Acts 13:3). The ministry of ordination was transmitted to disciples of the Apostles (see 1 Tim. 4:14, 2 Tim. 1:6), thus preserving the apostolic succession of the Church to the present day.

Deacons, presbyters, and bishops are officers of the Church. A future clergyman has the choice either of marrying or of remaining single. There are married and unmarried deacons and presbyters. Bishops, however, are elected from among unmarried priests. They are free from family cares so that they may be wholeheartedly devoted to the service of the Church. The supreme governing body of the Greek Orthodox Church and of the Eastern Orthodox Church is the totality of the bishops known as the synod, which professes Jesus as its head.

The Orthodox Church today favors and practices optional celibacy. But canon law rules that the individual who plans to enter the priesthood must decide before ordination whether he desires to serve the Church as a married man or as a celibate. Once a decision is made, he is expected to honor it and to stay in the status he chooses. No marriage is permitted after ordination, and no second marriage is allowed a priest who has lost a wife through either death or divorce. Widowers who are elected to the episcopal office usually are without children, or have only grown-up children.

In the Apostolic Church there were married and unmarried clergymen: deacons (1 Tim. 3:12), priests, and bishops (Tit. 1:5–6; 1 Tim. 3:2, 4–5). There were married and celibate Apostles. Among the twelve, only John seems to have been single, and after him, Saint Paul. There was no distinction between married and unmarried Apostles. In the great controversies between the Apostolic Church and the Gnostic sects concerning the morality of marriage and the value of celibacy, the Church eventually adopted a position which may be described as moderate, in full agreement with the Bible, socially pragmatic, and realistic.

By the middle of the seventh century there were still married and unmarried deacons, presbyters, and bishops. Until the first quarter of the sixth century, there was no discrimination against married bishops and no distinction between married and unmarried candidates for the espiscopate. In fact, there were canons protecting married bishops.

The fifth of the Apostolic Canons states that any bishop (or presbyter or deacon) who dismisses his wife on account of piety (or the pretence of piety) is to be defrocked or even excommunicated. Saint Paul's advice that "a bishop must be above reproach, the husband of one wife, temperate, sensible, dignified, hospitable, an apt teacher" (1 Tim. 3:2) was faithfully reiterated and respected. In the Greek Church, it was not rare for men who had married to be elevated to the ecumenical throne. For example, the patriarchs of Constantinople Manuel I (1217–1222), Joseph I (1268–1275), John XII Kosmas (1294–1303), and John XIII Glykes (1316–1320) had been married.

The celibate episcopate prevailed after the Synod of Trullo (691–692), not only because of the increasing influence of monastic ideals, but also because of the many responsibilities that preoccupy a married priest and as a reaction against nepotism, which tended to create problems within the Church. There was no theological argument against a married episcopate. Notwithstanding the practical advantages of a celibate episcopate, marriage was viewed as an honorable state for all three priestly ranks. As late as the twelfth century there were married bishops (married laymen, who, upon ordination, had refused to send their wives to convents as had been prescribed by the synod of Trullo, Canons 12 and 48). Emperor Isaak Angelos (1185–1195, 1203–1204) issued a law against this practice. In the Eastern Church, celibacy was never considered a prerequisite for ordination to any one of the priestly ranks. The canons did not impose upon or violate the free choice of the candidate for the priesthood.

Marriage after ordination, second marriages for widowed priests, and married bishops are questions of great concern to the Church today. Many theologians today believe that the Church could and should make changes relevant to contemporary needs. The movement in the Orthodox Church of Greece for a married clergy, including bishops, began as early as the reorganization of the Church in the early nineteenth century. Adamandios Koraes, one of the great intellectuals of nineteenth-century Hellenism, for example, advocated a married clergy and viewed the monastery as the place for celibates and monks. Action upon these issues rests not, however, with individual hierarchs or theologians, but with the whole Orthodox Church convened in an ecumenical or pan-Orthodox synod.

COLLABORATORS WITH THE CREATOR

Marriage is considered one of the most important sacraments of the Orthodox Church. The doctrinal foundations of matrimony are found in Holy Scripture and divine tradition, which constitute the continuous conscience of the Church. The Orthodox Church sees God himself as the source of every mystery in the Christian faith, including marriage. What procreates and perpetuates life cannot be anything but a mystery. As God created the first family, so God's agency, the Church, perpetuates God's creative concern for every new family. The Church as God's agent of grace unites man and woman, making them a microcosmic, or a miniature, Church—*"ten kat'oikon ecclesian"* (Rom. 16:5; cf. 1 Cor. 16:19).

Matrimony as an act of creation by God was raised to sacramental status by Christ and His Church. It is an event in which

God imparts invisible grace, through the Church, to two people as a twofold being. Marriage includes three basic interrelated elements: the natural element, which leads a man and a woman into a physical union; the moral element, which guarantees their full and perpetual cohabitation until death parts them; and the religious element, which makes marriage a communion of faith and a communion of two souls who decide to follow one road in life, a road that leads to virtue on earth and eternal salvation after physical death. This definition of marriage corresponds to the psychosomatic nature of man. "For this reason a man shall leave his father and mother and be joined to his wife, and the two shall become one" (Eph. 5:31). "So they are no longer two but one. What therefore God has joined together, let no man put asunder" (Mt. 19:6).

The sacramental character of matrimony, which was codified by the canon law of the Church, is based of course on other biblical testimony, explicit or implicit. The Bible states that God made man male and female; woman was made from the flesh of man, to be a companion of man, so that together they might continue the work of God by the procreation of mankind, multiply the human creatures of God, and have dominion upon the earth. Matrimony, which unites two human beings in order to produce a new creation, cannot but be a holy act. This intimate relationship of man and woman expresses God's continuous creative work. The human shares in the creativity and omnipotence of the Creator. Marriage is not a contract between two individuals but a sacred and creative union, the consummation of two human beings into one twofold being—a new "Adam-Eve" person.

Since the origin of matrimony is divine, its purpose too is sacred. Both Holy Scripture and sacred tradition reveal a threefold purpose: The first is to continue the creative work that God inaugurated with the creation of the first man and woman, thus propagating the human species. The second is to provide physical and moral assistance to two individuals who have placed themselves willingly under the same yoke. It is significant that in the Orthodox Church marriage is described as *syzygia*—partnership under a common yoke—which implies equal rights and responsibilities in the same household. The third purpose of marriage is summarized by Saint Paul in the following words:

> Because of the temptation to immorality, each man should have his own wife and each woman her own husband. The husband should give to his wife her conjugal rights, and likewise the wife to her husband. For the wife does not rule over her own body, but the husband does; likewise the husband does not rule over his own body, but the wife does.
>
> (1 Cor. 7:2–4)

Saint Paul speaks of sexual fulfillment in marriage as a major purpose of matrimony, a fulfillment that results from the union of two halves of the human person into one being. To paraphrase Saint John Chrysostom: The whole has no need to unite with anything, because it is complete, but two halves seek to unite with each other in order to become a whole. "Each half separately is imperfect."

Sexual intercourse is described in the Bible as "knowing." This means that conjugal union is more than a momentary union for hedonistic purposes; it is the result of thoroughly knowing each other, of deeply loving each other, of identifying the two lives one with another: they become one life in two persons. Marital sexuality has been elevated to a sacrament, and it is treated as a precious, beautiful, and holy gift that God gives as a reward to two heterosexual beings who place themselves under God's law in order to procreate and continue God's creativity. The relationship between husband and wife must not remain simply a state of knowing or being, but a continuous becoming. Their ultimate goal is to achieve the state of deification, for they are under the grace of God in a dynamic process, in a constant *gignesthai*, or becoming.

In the Orthodox Church, sexual intercourse is described as *synousia*, which means community of essence, consubstantiality. The use of such a profound theological term to describe the intimate relationship of husband and wife reveals the seriousness with which the Orthodox Church treats marriage and sexual intercourse.

On the other hand, celibacy is not considered an abnormality. The experience of the Church reveals that one can live a very happy and fulfilling life as a celibate. Celibacy and abstention from sexual intercourse, especially for religious purposes, can be found in the religious practices of the Greek, Roman, Semitic, and other peoples of antiquity.

The demand for celibacy in the Christian Church arose for several reasons. The enthusiastic and eschatological expectations of the early Church, and the prevailing concept of sexuality in Greco-Roman and Jewish society, influenced Christian thought. For example, the believers known as "enthusiasts" insisted that marriage was contrary to the teaching and primarily the example of Jesus. Some of them even went so far as to insist on celibacy as a prerequisite for the baptism of adults. The eschatological teachings of the early Church stressed that Christians are "strangers" and "pilgrims" on earth (1 Pet. 2:11; cf. Heb. 11:13) and encouraged the idea of celibacy. The expectation of the Lord's return made the creation of a family and family concerns unnecessary.

But against these views there arose many Church Fathers, from as early as the apostolic age, who saw the married state as the normal way for all Christians, laymen and clergymen alike. Religious celibacy is holy, but Christian marriage is holier.

The fact that the Church has not made an official pronouncement placing celibacy above marriage indicates that the conscience of the Church has accepted marriage as a more courageous state of being. While the celibate is expected not to cross a forbidden line, one who is married is exposed to more trials and temptations. Indeed, the way to moral perfection is harder and more demanding for the married than for the celibate.

The Orthodox tradition has accepted both marriage and celibacy under God as holy states as long as one honors the rights and restrictions of the state he is in. For example, Clement of Alexandria, born about 150, and writing about 194, stressed that to abstain from sexual intercourse is not virtuous in itself unless it is done for the sake of God, as Saint Paul had advised. He rebuked a group of heretics who described conjugal relations as unclean, and dissolved the arguments of another group of heretics who boasted that they believed in celibacy because Christ himself was celibate. Clement writes that Jesus was celibate indeed, but His Celibacy corresponded to the nature of Christ the God-man.

Christ, according to Clement, taught the sanctity and blessedness of celibacy when it is received as a gift of God for a particular ministry. In marriage, the whole human personality has been sanctified, "not only the spirit, but the ways and manners, the body and its total life."

Many Church Fathers recognized that it is possible for an individual Christian to live a sexual life with his wife and give heed to prayer at the same time. That is, they saw no contradiction between the life of the spirit and the needs of the body.

From the fourth century on, the Eastern Church demanded that the two partners in a marriage should be of the same Orthodox creed. Marriage with a non-Christian was forbidden and if contracted was declared illegal. She forbade marriage with heretics as well, while she was tolerant of marriage with schismatics. While in theory mixed marriages with infidels and with heretics were forbidden, in practice there were numerous mixed marriages between Orthodox and heretics as well as between Orthodox and non-Christians, especially among members of the imperial families and the upper classes. Mixed marriages multiplied after the tenth century and were rather common after the thirteenth. The Orthodox Church applied the principle of *oikonomia* (a judgment according to circumstances and needs) to holy matrimony more than to any other sacrament.

As late as the second half of the nineteenth century the Ecumenical Patriarchate in Constantinople (Istanbul), which set the pace for all autocephalous churches and Orthodox patriarchates to follow, forbade mixed marriages, on the basis of the canons of the ecumenical synods. An Orthodox person who marries a non-Orthodox outside the rules of the Church is denied the sacrament of Holy Communion. But a priest might be permitted to administer the sacrament in time of emergency.

Despite the earlier opposition of the Church, mixed marriages are allowed today between Orthodox and non-Orthodox Christians. Nevertheless, certain conditions must be borne in mind. The non-Orthodox member must agree:

(1) to be married by an Orthodox priest and

    (2) to have his or her children baptized and nurtured
       in the Orthodox faith.

The local bishop has the authority to exercise his right of *oikonomia*. Through *oikonomia* numerous mixed marriages were recognized during the seventeenth century and later.

The Orthodox Church opposes the dissolution of marriage save "for the cause of fornication" (Mt. 5:32), because the two partners have become one flesh. This is the ideal, which is not always observed. In the course of centuries, the Church has modified her teachings, and divorce is granted today on several other grounds, such as desertion, extreme cruelty, incompatibility, impotence, or incurable mental illness.

Like divorce, birth control has also been a controversial subject, and opinions differ among Orthodox theologians. No decision on birth control has been made by the ecumenical Orthodox Church. There are certain independent Orthodox jurisdictions or autocephalous churches that have taken a definite stand, condemning all methods of contraception, but their views have not been codified and are not binding upon all the Orthodox. Theological opinions expressed by societies, individual bishops, or scholars are not rare.

The Church of Greece, and likewise the Romanian Church, have issued special encyclicals condemning birth control. But the Church of Russia differs. V. Palachkovsky, of the Moscow Patriarchate, has said that "the whole domain of the relations between husband and wife . . . is too intimate to provoke the investigations of the priests," who serve as confessors and represent the Church.

The Ecumenical Patriarchate has left the matter to the discretion of husbands and wives in consultation with their priests. The late Patriarch Athenagoras is reported to have said: "Our Church has granted full authority to the spiritual father. It is for him, conscious of his responsibility and his mission, to give the advice and the direction that are appropriate."

It seems that the majority of the Orthodox faithful practice some form of birth control. In the past the matter was left to the responsibility of the father confessor, who advised his flock; but, with the decline of the practice of confession and spiritual direction, the matter has largely been left to each married couple. Even in circumstances that allow more open communication between couples and their priests, the priest seldom asks questions about this delicate matter. Thus, the ultimate decision rests with the faithful rather than with the clergy. Since there is no specific doctrine, canon, or consensus of teaching in the Orthodox Church at large against birth control, personal conscience, medical advice, and spiritual guidance determine a couple's attitude toward birth control.

While the Church is rather lenient, humanitarian, considerate, and practical with regard to divorce and birth control, she is unanimous and definite in the matter of abortion. Once life is conceived, a couple has no right to destroy it. On the contrary, the partners must rejoice and see it as a divine gift. Canon law has equated abortion with murder: "Those who give drugs for procuring abortion and those who receive poisons to kill the fetus are subject to the penalty of murder."

Respect and love for life underlies the whole concept of the teaching against abortion. Whether life is kept in a body ninety years old or developed in a fetus, it is life—the spirit of God and the dynamics of creation. However, when the survival of the mother is in question, the Orthodox believe that primary consideration should be given to her. The spouses are bound to follow their doctor's advice when abortion may be necessary. But, even under unavoidable circumstances, the Church imposes certain disabilities upon the mother for a certain period of time: she may not receive Holy Communion, for example, for a few months or even years. But, once again, it depends on the relationship between the spouses and their spiritual father, who is there to pray, advise, console, and guide the faithful. Admittedly, not all Christian families are close to a spiritual father and many of them follow the dictates of their conscience.

FOR THE HEALTH OF BODY AND SOUL

A neglected but vital aspect of Church life is the practice of holy unction. It is a sacrament primarily for the sick and is considered a healing service. It is based on the well-known passage in the Scriptures: "Is any among you sick? Let him call for the elders [presbyters] of the church, and let them pray over him, anointing him with oil in the name of the Lord; and the prayer of faith will save the sick man" (Js. 5:14).

The sacrament of holy unction is intended for the healing of the body and soul. Emphasis is placed on the close relationship between body and soul. The human being, as a psychosomatic entity, places itself at the mercy of Christ. If Christ was both the physician of the human soul and the healer of man's body, as the Gospels describe Him, then His Church cannot be anything less. Matthew's account of Jesus' ministry of healing is taken very seriously. Matthew writes: "And Jesus went about all the cities and villages . . . healing every disease and every infirmity" (9:35). Matthew adds that Christ, having summoned His disciples, gave them power over unclean spirits, to cast them out, and to cure every kind of disease and infirmity (10:1). This charismatic attribute of Jesus was transmitted to His Church.

The Orthodox Church today practices this ministry of healing, but to a limited degree and on special occasions. On the basis of other Biblical evidence, the Church stresses repentance and faith as prerequisites for the sacrament to have results. The disciples of Christ, the first Church, "went out and preached that men should repent. And they cast out many demons, and anointed with oil many that were sick and healed them" (Mk. 6:13). Notwithstanding the apostolic origin of this service, the Orthodox have relaxed its practice, and for the majority of the faithful, it is a once-a-year service. Of all the sacraments of the Church, sacred confession and holy unction are the least frequently practiced.

In addition to the liturgies or eucharistic services and the sacramental rites, there are several other practices directed to a variety of spiritual and physical needs of the faithful and commemorating great events in the life of the Church. Among these are the blessing of the waters on Epiphany Day, the exaltation of the holy cross, matins, vespers, the small and the great supplicatory services.

The cycles of these liturgies, sacraments, and services reveal that in its development in the course of the centuries Orthodoxy has intended to embrace the totality of human life and not remain simply abstract theology. Participating in the celebration of the Divine Liturgy, the sacrament of baptism, or the service of holy unction is a redemptive experience that makes God's presence real; that is to say, the participant has a feeling that the "metaphysical", or supernatural, is experienced. The doctrine, worship, and religious traditions of the Orthodox Church reveal that Orthodoxy claims the totality of man's life and sees the world as one arena for the religious enterprise.

In the sense of mystery, personal longings that individuals need satisfied are fulfilled. But not all respond to this type of religious experience, which on the whole is a personal rather than a social experience. The mystery's purpose is not only to convey the sense of purification, redemption, and delivery from sin, but knowledge of God as well, to make the initiate a friend of God and a participant in God for "in him we live and move and have our being" (Acts 17:28). This beautiful and most fulfilling concept was of ancient Greek origin and was used by Saint Paul in his address to the Athenians. Eventually it was incorporated into Christian mystical theology.

3

The Historical Development of Greek Orthodoxy

The Greek Orthodox Church today comprises five administrative jurisdictions: the Ecumenical Patriarchate of Constantinople (now Istanbul); the Patriarchates of Alexandria and Jerusalem, and the Churches of Cyprus and Greece. All together, the Church counts a membership of approximately fifteen million people living in Greece proper, the Near East, Africa, North and South America, Western Europe, and Australia. (It has been estimated that there are more than 150 million Orthodox Christians in the world. In a recent article in the *New York Times* the estimate was placed in the area of 300 million.) The Churches of Alexandria and Jerusalem include many thousands of Arabic-speaking Christians.

Greek and Greek-speaking Christians constituted the greater part of the early Church. With the diffusion of Hellenism, as early as the fourth century before the Christian era, the Greeks had come to constitute a very important if not a dominant element in the Near East and North Africa, especially in the large and metropolitan cities. It was because of this Greek world expansion that the rise of Christianity as a world religion was made possible.

The Greek Orthodox Church of today claims that she is the Church founded by Jesus Christ himself; that that Church was guided by the Apostles, including Saint Paul, who visited many

Greek cities, was strengthened by martyrs, saints, and the Church Fathers, and is maintained and propagated by her believers in the modern world.

The first contact of the Greeks with Christ is related by the author of the Fourth Gospel. He writes that some Greeks among those who used to visit Jerusalem at the Passover approached Philip and Andrew and asked to see Jesus (Jn. 12:20–24). The Greeks, as seekers after truth, were eager to listen to something novel, to meet the new master.

Since the dawn of history the Greeks have been inveterate wanderers in their search for the truth that sets man free. They have always been cosmopolitan and eager to attend one teacher after the other. Homer's Odysseus and Nikos Kazantzakis' Odysseus represent the restless Greek who, whether for knowledge, wealth, or truth, visits many lands and attends many schools of thought and learning. What Thucydides writes about the Athenians, describing them as a people that "could neither rest themselves nor permit others to rest," can be said of all the Ancient Greeks.

Jesus was aware that the Greeks who came to Him were men with a searching mind and a troubled spirit. Upon His confrontation with them, He exclaimed, "The hour has come for the son of man to be glorified" (Jn. 12:23). Indeed, these Greeks were few in number, but Christ saw in them not only Greeks but Romans and Scythians and other peoples of all times and places who would also seek to find Him. Jesus said the hour had come for the Christian Gospel to be proclaimed outside the limited boundaries of ancient Israel. The Greeks have played a major role in the *kerygma* and the *didache* of Christ. The Greeks found in the person of Christ the eternal Logos and the "unknown God" of their forefathers, while Christ discovered in them sincere followers and dedicated apostles of the new kingdom. It was through this historical meeting between the "unknown God" and the Greeks themselves that Christianity became an ecumenical religion. As T. R. Glover has put it: "The chief contribution of the Greek was his demand for this very thing—that Christianity must be universal ... the Greek really secured the triumph of Jesus. ... Even the faults of the Greek have indirectly served the church." Thus Christianity and Hellenism embraced each other in a harmonious faith and culture, enriching each other, saving each other for eternity. The Greek Orthodox Church of today is the people born out of the union between the incarnate Logos and Hellenism.

In the history of the Greek Orthodox Church four stages of development can be distinguished. The first three centuries, through the age of Constantine the Great, constitute the apostolic and ancient period. The medieval period includes almost ten centuries, to the fall of Constantinople. The age of captivity starts, roughly, in the fifteenth century and ends about the year 1830. It is followed by the modern period.

The Ancient Church

Soon after its inception, Christianity was promulgated in the Greek-speaking world of the Roman Empire. It was propagated through the medium of the Greek language; it was interpreted and clarified by the Fathers of Christianity, who were either Greek in origin or Hellenized and who spoke and wrote in Greek. Christian creeds and canons were written and codified in the Greek language by local and ecumenical synods as well. The New Testament books themselves and much of the important literature of the Christian religion of the first ten centuries were written in Greek. Greek philosophical thought and learning were utilized in defining Christian doctrines. Even Western Church Fathers such as Jerome, Ambrose, and Augustine, who wrote in the Latin language, reveal the influence of Greek thought in their writings.

Following three centuries of underground existence and persecution in the Roman Empire, it was again the Greek Church, the Greek language, and Greek missionaries that carried the Christian message in both the East and the West. The Latin element emerged as a major factor in the history of Christianity only in the West and as late as the fifth century. It is significant that Saint Paul, writing to the Church of Rome, did not use Latin but Greek. The early Church in Rome was Greek-speaking. Christianity is Greek not only in form but to a great degree in content as well. As we have seen, Greek religious and philosophical thought had penetrated into the mind and thought of later Judaism. The influence of Hellenism on the intellects of the Jews was very strong—if not all-pervasive—for more than three centuries.

Orthodox and non-Orthodox Christian theologians agree on the close relationship between Christianity and Greek thought. The late Russian-American theologian Georges Florovsky observes that "Hellenism has placed its eternal character upon the Church. It has become an inseparable part of her very being and as such every Christian is, to some extent, a Hellene. Hellenism is not simply a phase in the history of Christianity but a cornerstone in its life. . . . There is no Catholic Christian theology outside of Hellenism." Florovsky refers, of course, to the period of Christian antiquity, which developed under the influence of the Greek language, thought, piety, mysticism, and ethos. Christianity and Hellenism emerged as a new synthesis in the Greek East and the Latin West of the Roman Empire.

A. Cleveland Coxe, editor of the American edition of the Ante-Nicene Fathers Series, wrote about the Greek character of early Christianity: "Primitive Christianity was Greek in form and character, Greek from first to last, Greek in all its forms of dogma, worship and policy."

Arthur P. Stanley, a distinguished professor of ecclesiastical history at Oxford, some hundred years ago wrote in even more lively terms:

> The Greek Church reminds us of the time when the tongue, not of Rome, but of Greece, was the sacred language of Christendom. It was a striking remark of the Emperor Napoleon, that the introduction of Christianity itself was, in a certain sense, the triumph of Greece over Rome; the last and most signal instance of the maxim of Horace, *Graecia capta ferum victorem cepit* (captive Greece took its rude captor captive). The early Roman Church was but a colony of Greek Christians or Grecized Jews. The earliest Fathers of the Western Church wrote in Greek. The early popes were not Italians, but Greeks. The name of the pope is not Latin, but Greek, the common and now despised name of every pastor in the Eastern Church. . . . She is the mother and Rome the daughter. It is her privilege to claim a direct continuity of speech with the earliest times; to boast of reading the whole code of Scripture, Old as well as New, in the language in which it was

read and spoken by the Apostles. The humblest peasant who reads his Septuagint or Greek Testament in his mother-tongue on the hills of Boeotia may proudly feel that he has access to the original oracles of divine truth which pope and cardinal reach by a barbarous and imperfect translation: that he has a key of knowledge which in the West is only to be found in the hands of the learned classes.

Modern theologians echo Stanley's thesis. Hugo Rahner, a leading Roman Catholic theologian, adds that "God spoke his revelation into the world of the Greek spirit and the Roman imperium, and the Church guards this truth framed in the Greek speech of her sacred Book . . . . the Church will continue to speak Greek even if . . . Hellas descend into the abyss of utter oblivion." And Georges Florovsky adds: "The task of our time, in the Orthodox world, is to rebuild the Christian-Hellenic culture, not out of the relics and memories of the past, but out of the perennial spirit of our Church, in which the values of culture were truly christened. Let us be more Hellenic in order that we may be truly Christian." The Greek spirit and culture are permanently wedded to the Christian faith, neither of which can be separated from the other without deforming itself. Indeed, "the heritage of the Greek spirit only attains immortality within the shrine of the Logos whose words are recorded in the tongue of Hellas."

While Tertullian, the second-century Christian apologist, scornfully satirized those who "advocated a Stoic or a Platonic or a dialectic [Aristotelian] Christianity" and Christianity wrestled for several centuries with Tertullian's question, "What has Athens to do with Jerusalem?", Greek Christianity had achieved at an early age a balance between the wisdoms of two cities, the *thyrathen,* that is, the Hellenic, and the Sacred.

The early Church arrived at the conclusion that the study of Greek wisdom was both useful and desirable provided the Christian rejected evil and retained all that is good and true, "for the good wherever it is found is a property of the truth," as Socrates, the ecclesiastical historian, writes. But as a whole the Fathers and writers of the Greek Church did not seek to borrow essence and content from ancient Greek thought, for those they possessed in their sacred revelation. They sought to borrow methodologies, technical means, terminology, and logical or grammatical structures in order to build up the Christian edifice of theology, of doctrine, and thought.

As ancient Greek religion encompassed the whole of man and was concerned with the totality of man by having elaborate rituals for different occasions of his life—for rain and harvest, for the ill and the traveler—so the Orthodox Church is likewise very much concerned with the whole of man, body and soul. Thus she has rituals, prayers, and festivities for every significant event of man's life. As the ancient Greeks "never felt any limitation to their religious imagination and curiosity," likewise the Christian Greeks enjoy a variety of religious events and expressions.

Not only in good but even in bad traditions and practices there are striking similarities between the two Greek religious worlds. In ancient Greece, religion was subordinate to civil authority and the city-state was the supreme power, appointing priests as state officials and establishing and supervising temples, sacred groves, and altars. Likewise Orthodox Christianity has been subordinated again and again to civil authority, and often the state, whether in the Byzantine era, in "holy" Russia, in Romania, or in Greece, has exercised a tremendous influence upon the Church.

Furthermore, as the priests in ancient Greek religion were never the final religious authority, so the clergy in Orthodoxy are never the Church proper or the final arbiters in matters of faith, ethics, or even ecclesiastical administration. Even though Greek Orthodox Christianity subscribes to the Nicene-Constantinopolitan creed and to the doctrinal decisions of ecumenical synods, and at the surface may appear very conservative, if not stifling, the truth is that in practice there is in Greek Orthodoxy a tremendous variety of religious expression and freedom, similar to that of ancient Greece.

There have indeed been reactions against this Hellenic infiltration not only by Tertullian, Romanos the Melodist, and the Iconoclasts, but also by modern Greek Orthodox bishops, who have stressed the need to de-Hellenize and re-Judaicize Christianity. Historically, however, all such attempts have failed. Orthodox and non-Orthodox theologians and scholars believe that the Judaization of Christianity would have been fatal, while its Hellenization determined its universal appeal and its catholic character. Greek Orthodox Christianity is Christocentric and Biblical, but at the same time it bears all the characteristics of the Greek genius. Christianity's religious schemes and theological categories reveal the influence of the ancient Greek mind. There is unity, but a unity in diversity. There is canon law, but it is not always enforced. The concept of the Roman *auctoritas* has found little fertile ground in the Greek East. The Greek emphasis on inquiry and the continuous quest for personal understanding and interpretation constitute the background of the development of "heresies," or "choices," outside the mainstream of Orthodoxy.

The contrasts in religious styles and practices in Orthodoxy recall the contrasts in religious faiths and styles of life in the Greco-Roman world in which Christianity was born and nurtured. To be sure, there were magic and superstition and terror. But there was also "a lofty mysticism with keen critical insight and clear philosophical alignment and a high and unselfish morality." There was asceticism in ugly forms as there was an asceticism of self-denial, self-knowledge, and continuous striving for spiritual perfection. Asceticism and continence as ideals of holiness, and the longing for *soteria* (salvation) and *theosis* (deification), were adopted by early Christianity from Greek religious or philosophical practices, from Orphic, Pythagorean, Stoic, and Hermetic teachings and practices.

It is fashionable even among Greek Orthodox theologians to criticize this infiltration, the rational element and the academic arguments in Orthodox theology, and instead to stress either the simplistic Biblical, or the mystical and the apophatic approach. We would agree with a Protestant critic of the "de-Hellenizers" who writes: "If the Church had fully understood and accepted the purpose and spirit of Christ, the great rational Graeco-Roman civilization so far as we can see, need not have been swept away."

It was Paul who contributed greatly to the development of harmonious relations between Christianity and the Greeks. He visited and established Christian congregations in all the important Hellenic centers of the Asiatic continent and the

European mainland. He further explained the "unknown God," to whom the Greeks had erected numerous sanctuaries in such cities as Athens, Olympia, and Pergamum, and the Greeks did not hesitate to become his disciples. A distinguished historian of the Greek and Roman worlds, A. H. M. Jones, rightly observes that "the strength of early Christianity lay predominantly in Greek-speaking urban areas." The name "Christian" replaced the ethnic name of the Greeks for many centuries, while their national name, "Hellene," lost its original meaning.

Two factors contributed to this change. After Caracalla's edict in 212, all Greeks and members of other nationalities of the Roman Empire became Roman citizens. Thus, from the third century on the Greeks were referred to as Romans, or *Romeoi*. Furthermore, with the attempts of Emperor Julian to revive paganism, "Hellene," as an ethnic or national name, came to be identified with the ancient religious cults, the pagan gods, and the ancient classical tradition in general. *Hellene* and *Hellenismos* became synonymous with paganism. The Greeks were simply Christians of the Roman Empire. The designation "Christian" persists to a great degree even today. When a Greek inquires about someone he does not know, he usually asks not whether the person is a Greek but whether he or she is a Christian.

For historical and circumstantial reasons the Greeks for many centuries developed a supranational conscience and preferred to identify themselves solely as Christians, especially during the four hundred years of captivity under the Turks. It is significant that, although the patriarchs of Constantinople and many bishops of the Bulgarians, Albanians, Armenians, and Slavs were Greeks during the Ottoman period, they did not attempt to Hellenize their congregations; neither did they try to force them to abandon their liturgical traditions and cultures. Of course, every rule has its exceptions. The fact is, however, that the tradition of the Greek Church has been one of religious toleration rather than nationalism. If this had not been true, the Greek Church, in the Byzantine centuries and especially during the four hundred years under the Turks, could have Hellenized all the minorities under her aegis or at least a great majority of them. The Greek historian C. Paparrigopoulos, known for his patriotism, blamed the Church for not exploiting her numerous opportunities to Hellenize the various Balkan peoples in a period of four hundred years, something she could have done without much difficulty.

The term "Hellene" as an ethnic name began to appear among the Greeks of the high Middle Ages, but still was not commonly used. However, all nations living outside the medieval Greek world of the Byzantine Empire, such as the Russians, the Germans, the English, the peoples of Italy, and the Franks, called the native inhabitants of the Byzantine Empire "Greeks." The designations "Greek Orthodox" and "Roman Catholic" were unknown in the early and medieval Church, and they took on their distinct meanings only after the eleventh century.

Nevertheless, it was Greeks, or Hellenized missionaries, both those of the Asiatic dispersion and those of the European continent, who played a leading role in the history of Christianity. Antioch, Tarsos, Ephesos, Smyrna, Philippi, Thessaloniki, Athens, Corinth, Nicopolis, the islands of Cyprus and Crete, were only a few of the many Greek cities and territories that heard the Christian gospel. All the important churches of the first three centuries were Greek or Greek-speaking. Besides Saint Paul, other Apostles such as Andrew, John the Evangelist, Philip, Luke, Mark, and Titus, labored for the Christianization of the Greeks. As early as the second century there were flourishing churches not only in the cities just mentioned but also in such lesser Greek towns as Megara, Sparta, Patras, Larissa, Melos, Tenos, Paros, Thera, and Chios.

Many of these Greek cities produced great martyrs and profound thinkers during this period. Men such as Polycarp, Ignatios, Aristides, Athenagoras, Anakletos (bishop of Rome where he is listed as Anacletus), Clement of Alexandria, Origen, Gregory the Illuminator of the Armenians, Justin, and Melito of Sardis were either Greek or Hellenized; some were born in the city of Athens or educated there. On the other hand, the persecutions of the Christians under the Roman emperors Nero, Domitian, Trajan, Marcus, Aurelius, Galerius, and Diocletian affected the Greek East much more than the Western Roman Empire. Dionysios, bishop of Athens, Aristios of

Dyrrahio, Nikephoros, Cyprian, Dionysios, Anekitos, Parilos, Leonidas, Irene, Demetrios, Catherine, Zeno, Eusebios, Zotikos, and Theodoulos are only a few of the thousands of martyrs of such places as Corinth, Athens, Thessaloniki, Gortyn in Crete, Philippi, and Kercyra (Corfu). It was their blood that nourished the Christian seed, as Tertullian observed. The first period in the history of the Church ended with the edict of toleration in 313 under Constantine the Great, which prepared the way for Christianity to become the state religion of the later Roman and Byzantine empires.

The Medieval Church

Every student of history knows quite well the tremendous contributions of the Greeks to Christianity during the millennium of the Byzantine Empire. This was the period of the Greek Fathers, of immense missionary enterprises, of Christian thought, poetry, and literature. It was the period of local and ecumenical synods, which formed and defined the Christian faith basic to all Christian churches and denominations today. It was also an era of great social concern and cultural activity in the Church.

The Greek Orthodox today consider the following events as the chief landmarks of their medieval heritage. From the year 325 to 787, seven ecumenical synods were convened to discuss the common concerns of the universal Church: to define the Christian faith, to issue uniform canons, to plan their common destiny. The first and second ecumenical synods (Nicaea, 325, and Constantinople, 381) dealt with the Holy Trinity, while the third (Ephesos, 431) and fourth (Chalcedon, 451) dealt with the person of Jesus Christ.

It is true that most major heresies originated in the Greek East. But all of them were defeated on the same ground by the intellect, the logic, the mystical intuition, and the Biblical scholarship of the Greek Fathers, or their Hellenized allies of the Near East. The Christian West at that time was going through a period of crisis and readjustment and there was little room for intellectual curiosity, discussion, inquiry, or theological or philosophical speculation. Thus, indeed, very few heresies arose there. The Christian West was to produce its own great

Fathers, such as Jerome, Ambrose, and especially Augustine. But early Christian theology was the work of the Greek rather than the Latin mind.

The seventh ecumenical synod (Nicaea II, of 787), was again a victory of the Greek mind and Christian understanding over the Semitic and Oriental mind. Its decisions were reaffirmed by the synod of 843, which proclaimed the legitimate place of icons, symbols, and representations in Christian worship. In other synods, such as those during the episcopacy of Photios, the synodal and democratic administrative system of the Church was proclaimed, thus reaffirming the ancient apostolic tradition.

During this period there were several ecclesiastical centers that survive today as centers of Orthodoxy: Constantinople, Alexandria, Antioch, Jerusalem, and the island of Cyprus. With the exception of Antioch and Jerusalem, whose present-day Christians are Syrian and Arabic Orthodox, all the others maintain strong Greek-speaking Orthodox sees.

The great Church Fathers, theologians, monastics, and missionaries flourished during this same early medieval period. Basil the Great, Gregory of Nyssa, John Chrysostom, Athanasios, Cyril, Eusebios of Caesarea, Maximos the Confessor, Leontios Byzantios, Romanos Melodos, John of Damascus, Theodore Studites, Tarasios, John Eleemon, Photios, Cyril and Methodios, Nicholas Mystikos, Michael Kyrullarios, and Symeon the New Theologian are a few of the many churchmen who made Christianity a vital and redeeming force in the Middle Ages.

One cannot overemphasize the outstanding contributions of the Church of Constantinople in the propagation of the Christian faith to the peoples of Asia Minor as well as to those of Central and Eastern Europe. The Greek brothers Cyril and Methodios from Thessaloniki, apostles to the Slavs, were missionaries of culture and civilization as well as of religion.

Highly educated, Cyril and Methodios undertook to form a written alphabet for the Slav nations so as to translate the Bible and sacred books into their tongue, shape their worship, and enable them to adopt new ways of thinking and living. Bulgarians, Pannonians, Moravians, Czechs, Russians, and other tribes "rejoiced to hear the Greatness of God extolled in their native tongue," as the Russian *Primary Chronicle* puts it.

The Church manifested a brilliant social consciousness during this period. Saint Basil, John Chrysostom, John Eleemon, Justinian, Theophilos, Constantine IX, John II Komnenos, and many other churchmen and emperors inaugurated considerable social welfare programs, all of which were under the aegis of the Church. Hospitals, old-age homes, orphanages, reformatory institutions, hospices, leprosaria, and other philanthropic institutions were built next to churches and monasteries. The monastic communities of such cities and regions as Constantinople, Jerusalem, Alexandria, Athos, and Ephesos were great social forces in the work of the Church.

The development and cultivation of literature, art, and culture during the Middle Ages is another important chapter in the history of the Greek Church. Greek Church poetry is indeed brilliant and comprises many large volumes used in the Church today. Byzantine art, which is becoming more and more popular, is an achievement in itself. Monasteries were praying communities as well as working and artistic laboratories. The art of calligraphy, together with the transcription of the works of classical authors and Church Fathers, was strongly encouraged by the Church.

In brief, notwithstanding her shortcomings, and they were many, the Greek medieval Church was a very positive and constructive institution for the propagation of Christianity and the preservation of Greek and Roman culture. It was during this period, however, that Latin Christianity, which had been isolated for several centuries, broke away from its roots and its unity with Greek Christianity. The great schism was the result of many factors, linguistic, cultural, theological, and political.

It was the Western Church that estranged herself from the Eastern Church. Constantinople had been the capital of the Empire since A.D. 330. The city of Constantine was the commanding center of the *orbis Romanorum*. By abandoning old Rome and moving to the Greek East, Constantine indicated that the future of the empire lay in the East. The Byzantine Greeks almost ignored the developments in the Western Church, where the bishop of Rome was the sole patriarch.

True, the Eastern Church acknowledged and honored the bishop of the old capital as the first among equals (*primus inter pares*) in honor, but she did not consider him *Pontifex Maximus* (chief bishop) or vicar of Christ on earth.

Appeals to Rome from the clergy of the Eastern Church in disciplinary or theological matters were rare. When bishops were elected patriarchs of Eastern sees they did not ask for confirmation by the pope but simply announced their elevation and added their confession of faith in order to declare that their faith was the same as that of the first patriarchal see. The same announcement and declaration of faith or a very similar one were sent to each of the other patriarchs. Even Roman Catholic and other Western theologians and historians, such as Francis Dvornik and H. Grotz, acknowledge that the heads of the Eastern patriarchates acted independently in disciplinary matters in their jurisdictions. No Church rules existed that obliged the Eastern or Greek patriarchs to submit themselves to Rome before the ninth century. It was in the middle of the ninth century that the Roman pope made claims of supreme jurisdiction over all patriarchs and bishops of Christendom. But even those claims were formulated on the basis of spurious documents, the Pseudo-Isidorian Decretals. The strain in relations between the two parts of Christendom was intensified after the ninth century, when several powerful popes like Nicholas I (858–867) thought of extending to the East the authority they exercised in the West.

H. Grotz, an eminent contemporary Roman Catholic Church historian, analyzing the development of the papal primacy in Western Christendom, writes:

> In the West the extraordinary position of the Pope had relatively crystalized [in the ninth century] owing to the progress made by theological speculation, due to the Germanic devotional piety towards Rome, thanks also to the political development which promoted the Pope almost to a guardian of the imperial crown, but also thanks to the legend of Pope Sylvester, to the legendary Donation of Constantine and to the appearance of the Pseudo-Decretals.

But the Western understanding of the papacy was foreign to the Eastern mind, which believed that the supreme authority of the Church rested with the ecumenical synod and that the universal Church honored the heads of the five patriarchates above all other bishops, amongst whom the patriarch or pope of Rome was the first.

When disputes arose among the clergy of the Eastern Church, the ultimate authority was Constantinople, not Rome. The ninth canon of the fourth ecumenical synod (451) clearly prescribes:

> If any clergyman has a dispute with another . . . let him first submit his case to his own bishop, or let it be tried by referees chosen by both parties and approved by the bishop. Let anyone who acts contrary be liable to canonical penalties. If, on the other hand, a clergyman has a dispute with his own bishop or with some other bishop, let it be tried by the synod of the province. But if any bishop or clergyman has a dispute with the metropolitan of the same province, let him apply either to the exarch of the diocese or to the throne of the imperial capital Constantinople, and let it be tried before him.

The Eastern Church, whether in the past or in the present, has never accepted a patriarch or a pope as infallible. In fact, she has condemned some as heretics. For example, the third ecumenical synod (431) condemned Patriarch Nestorios for heresy, and the sixth ecumenical synod (681) condemned Pope Honorius for heresy.

In any case, after several confrontations between the Eastern and Western, or Greek and Latin, churches, there came a crisis in the year 1054, which is the traditional date of the great schism. The major problem in the dispute was the Roman claim to primacy in arbitrating all matters of faith, morals, and administration. The Greek East, which knew of no precedent for this claim, had refused to accept it. The Orthodox position toward the Roman claims can be found in the answer of Niketas, archbishop of Nikomedia, to Anselm, bishop of Havelberg, in the twelfth century. To several accusations of Anselm's, Niketas responded as follows:

> My dearest brother, we do not deny to the Roman Church the primacy amongst the five sister patriarchates [Rome, Constantinople, Alexandria, Antioch, and Jerusalem], and we recognize her right to the most honorable seat at an ecu-

menical synod. But, she has separated herself from us by her own deeds, when through pride she assumed a monarchy which does not belong to her office. . . . How shall we accept decrees from her that have been issued without consulting us and even without our knowledge? If the Roman pontiff, seated on the lofty throne of his glory, wishes to thunder at us and, so to speak, hurl his mandates at us and our churches, not by taking counsel with us but at his own arbitrary pleasure, what kind of brotherhood or even what kind of parenthood can this be? We would be the slaves not the sons of such a church, and the Roman see would not be the pious mother of sons but a hard and imperious mistress of slaves. . . . In such a case what could have been the use of the scriptures? The writings and the teachings of the Fathers would be useless. The authority of the Roman pontiff would nullify the value of all because he would be the only bishop, the sole teacher and master.

The two worlds were further divided as a result of the barbarism of the Crusaders and the brutalities they inflicted upon the Greek East. The Crusaders' "macabre expression of a pagan death wish," in the words of a modern Western historian, brought the final rupture between Roman Catholicism and Greek Orthodoxy. The fall of Constantinople to the Crusaders in 1204 marked the beginning of the end of the medieval period of the Greek Church, which then entered into her darkest centuries.

With the fall of Constantinople to the Ottoman Turks in 1453, the Greek Orthodox Church became a "nation" under the Turks. At the beginning the Church seemed to thrive under the privileges that were granted her by the conqueror Mohammed II. The patriarch and actually every bishop in his own diocese were invested with religious and civil powers, and each one of them became the spokesman of his flock.

The ecumenical patriarch of Constantinople, as well as the heads of other autocephalous, or self-governing, churches, came to be known as "ethnarchs," a title that the archbishop of Cyprus retains today, and that denotes the religious and national spokesmen of their constituents. However, the ecumenical patriarch, who had been acknowledged as the "first among equals" in the East, became the most important religious leader of all Christians under the Turks. A few of them proved unworthy hierarchs, but others rose above the temptations, the corruption, and the pressures of the sultan as worthy representatives and even martyrs.

Many patriarchs and other clerics of the Orthodox Church who refused to obey the whim of the sultans were dethroned or exiled or in most cases put to death. A few cases may suffice to substantiate this point. Joachim I (1504) was dethroned; Cyril Loukaris (1638), Cyril Kontaris (1639), Parthenios II (1504), Parthenios III (1657), Gregory V (1821), and others were put to death. Neophytos V (1707) was thrown into the galleys, and several others, such as Jeremias II (1769), Athimos III (1824), Chrysanthos (1826), and Agathagelos (1830) were exiled. In addition to heavy taxation of the Christians, as well as insults and arbitrary actions on the part of the Turkish autocracy, the Church suffered from confiscation of its houses of worship and property, and Christians were forced to deny their faith and adopt the Moslem religion.

Notwithstanding many outbreaks of Islamic fanaticism during those four centuries, the Greek Church manifested a great deal of vitality. No epoch that produces martyrs can be described as morbid and corrupt. In particular during the sixteenth and seventeenth centuries, many Orthodox witnessed to their faith "unto death." The Greek Church commemorates the names of many neomartyrs, who preferred to die rather than deny their Christian faith, among them Michael Mauroides, Gabriel II, Theodore of Mytilene, Christodoulos, Cyril of Thessalonica (burned alive in July 1566, at the age of 22), Mark Kyriakopolos (beheaded in 1643 at Smyrna), John (put to death in 1652, at the age of 14)—172 in all.

Objective information about all of this has been transmitted not only through Greek primary sources, but through the observations of Western travelers or civil servants who served in various cities of the Ottoman Empire. For example, the British consul Paul Ricaut, stationed in Smyrna, wrote about 1678 a vivid account of the state of the Greek and the Armenian churches under the Turks.

> The increase and prevalency of the Christian faith against the violence of kings and emperors, and all the terrors of

death, is a demonstration of its verity; so the stable perseverance in these our days [i.e., 1678] of the Greek Church
therein, notwithstanding the oppression and contempt put
upon it by the Turk, and the allurements and pleasures of
this world, is a confirmation no less convincing than the mir-
acles and power which attended its first beginnings: for indeed it is admirable to see and consider with what Constancy,
Resolution, and Simplicity, ignorant and poor men kept their
Faith; and that the proffer of worldly preferments and the
privilege which they enjoy by becoming Turks, the mode and
Fashion of that country which they inhabit . . . would have
induced the Greeks to denounce their faith.

Ricaut adds that much of their perseverance "is to be attributed
to the grace of God and the promises of the gospel."

On the one hand the Greek Church suffered from the Turkish and Islamic oppression and persecution, and on the other,
she also suffered from the propaganda, the intrigues, and the
proselytizing activities of the Jesuits, the Capuchins, the
Uniates, and several Protestant denominations. Paul Ricaut
adds:

But not only hath the *Greek* Church the *Turk* for an enemy
and an oppressor, but also the Latines; who not being able
by their missionaries to gain them to their party, and per-
suade them to renounce the jurisdiction of their Patriarchs,
and own the authority and supremacy of the Roman Bishop,
do never omit those occasions which may bring them under
the lash of the Turk, and engage them in a constant and
continual expense, hoping that the people being oppressed
and tyred, and in no condition of having relief under the
protection of their own Governors, may at length be induced
to embrace a foreign Head, who hath riches and power to
defend them. Moreover, besides their wiles, the Roman
priests frequent all places, where the Greeks inhabit, en-
deavoring to draw them unto their side both by preachings
and writings.

On account of this the late British scholar A. H. Hore of Trinity
College, Oxford, observed: "The fall of the Eastern Empire
and the low state to which the persecuted Greek Church fell,
and from which it is little less than a miracle that it should now

be recovering, is a chapter of dishonor and disgrace in the history of Western Europe."

No doubt the Greek Church found herself between various adversaries whose only objective was to convert her faithful to their own creeds. However, much decay originated from within the administration of the Church herself. Simony, quarrels, and poverty among the clergy contributed to the already low state of the Church. I agree with several modern historians who believe that "the survival of the Greek Church under four centuries of Turkish rule is no less than a miracle."

The Greek Orthodox Church is not to be confused with the "Greek" Catholic Church, which is a branch of the Roman Church. In fact, the Church of Rome includes members of the Byzantine Rite. The Orthodox on the other hand, who commonly use the name "Greek Catholic," use it always with other attributes such as Russian Orthodox Greek Catholic, Carpatho-Russian Orthodox Greek Catholic, etc. "Greek Catholic" alone refers to the Roman branch of Greek liturgical background, also known as "Uniate," i.e., in union with the Roman Catholic Church.

There are several major differences between the Orthodox and the Roman churches, including the following: The primacy and the infallibility of the Roman pope; the *Filioque* clause, that is, the teaching concerning the procession of the Holy Spirit from the Son; the teachings on purgatory, and on the immaculate conception and the bodily assumption of the Theotokos (Mary the God-bearer). All these are rejected by the Orthodox. In addition there are other doctrinal, ecclesiastical, and administrative differences between the Orthodox and the Latin Churches. The Greek Church recognizes only a primacy of honor due the bishop of Rome, the bishop of Constantinople, and other Church leaders, for historical reasons. The institution of the Roman papacy as it evolved in the West after the ninth century was foreign to the early Church; thus it has never been accepted in the East. The development of the Roman primacy was one of the major causes of the schism between the Latin West and the Greek East, and it continues to be a stumbling block for the reunion of Christendom, since it has become an element of the doctrinal teaching of the Roman Catholic faith. No doubt the idea of the primacy of the bishop of Rome is in harmony with the Roman imperial tradition, but in Orthodox eyes it is alien to the teaching of Christ and the early Church. The Roman Catholic Church after Charlemagne transformed the primacy of honor into a primacy of leadership and authority, and the bishop of Rome claimed to be the *Pontifex Maximus* over all Christendom. These claims brought about the rupture between the Latin West and the Greek East in the eleventh century.

Both the New Testament books and the documents of the late first and early second centuries support the Orthodox teaching that the early Church was governed by a board or a synod of bishops. Christ entrusted His gospel to the Apostles, and the Apostles "appointed their successors . . . to be bishops . . . of those who were to receive the faith," as Saint Clement of Rome writes. A work of visions called *The Shepherd of Hermas*, written in the first half of the second century, speaks about "those who rule the Church of Rome . . . and the presbyters who are set over the Church."

Another Father of the Church, Saint Cyprian, bishop of Carthage (248–258), points out that "the episcopal office and the organization of the Church have come down to us so that the Church is founded upon the bishops and every act of the Church is controlled by these same officers." He further emphasizes that all the bishops are equal in rank and authority. He adds that "neither does any of us [bishops] set himself up as a bishop of bishops, nor by tyrannical terror does any compel his colleague to the necessity of obedience. . . . Our Lord Jesus Christ . . . is the only one that has the power of preferring us [the bishops] as the government of His Church." Cyprian's views about the equality of the bishops in the early Church were shared by other writers of the first three centuries. Firmilian, bishop of Caesarea (*c.*256) is another witness to this principle.

But even in the West each bishop was essentially independent of higher ecclesiastical authority, and only after the ninth century is there a strong tendency on the part of the bishop of Rome to assert himself over the rest of the bishops, who, because of their weakness, needed protection from some strong political or ecclesiastical leader. Political circumstances contributed to the emergence of a supreme ecclesiastical authority in Western Christendom. Unification under an effective head, who could exercise authority over all the clergy and protect them from secular lords, became desirable. The papacy, as it is understood today, appears essentially in the eleventh century, when it was strengthened especially by the activities of the Clunaic movement, which aspired to see the Church united and purified under a central bishop—the pope of Rome.

It should be emphasized that as long as the Roman Catholic Church teaches the supremacy in authority and power of the bishop of Rome over all Christendom, there is little hope for progress in the ecumenical dialogue on the reunion of the Churches. The Orthodox Church would have no hesitation in accepting the bishop of Rome as the *primus inter pares,* the first among equals. But she would yield no other ground on that important subject.

There were several trends in medieval Greek Christianity which to some degree persist to the present day. There is evangelical and fundamentalist Orthodox Christianity, emphasizing traditionalism and biblicism as the major criteria of Orthodoxy. This has been the faith of the monks, the conservative clergy, and the common folk, and it can be traced back to theologians like Anastasios Sinaites, John Chrysostom, Theodore Studites, and others. Mysticism has nurtured several independent minds and has been a powerful trend in Orthodoxy from as early as the Byzantine era. In the persons of Maximos the Confessor, Symeon the New Theologian, Gregory Palamas, and Nicholas Kabasilas, Orthodox mysticism was developed into a profound theology that has become the subject of many studies in recent years. But we have more to say on mysticism in another chapter.

The Modern Church

The modern period in the history of the Greek Church begins with the liberation of a considerable segment of the Hellenic world from the Turks in 1832. To the five autocephalous (self-governing) Greek-speaking Orthodox Churches of that time, namely, the Ecumenical Patriarchate of Constantinople, the

Patriarchates of Alexandria, Antioch, and Jerusalem, and the Church of Cyprus, there was added the autocephalous Church of Greece.

The Ecumenical Patriarchate, with jurisdiction over the Greek Orthodox of Western Europe, North and South America, Australia, and several islands of Greece, has a membership of approximately three and a half million faithful. The ecumenical patriarch, who heads it, is respected by all Orthodox as the first among equals and serves as the strongest link of unity among all Orthodox. Despite harassment by Turkish governments in the past decade or so, the Patriarchate remains the most important citadel in all Orthodoxy. Until very recently it maintained an excellent theological school, and its initiative in and contributions to the ecumenical movement are outstanding examples of a progressive, albeit suffering, Church.

Among the outstanding contributions of the Ecumenical Patriarchate in recent years, several deserve our attention. Many endeavors have been undertaken to bring into closer cooperation all the autocephalous Orthodox Churches of the world. The Patriarchate aspires to establish a federation of all Orthodox churches and to make their spiritual unity visible in their administrative cooperation. The recent pan-Orthodox synods on the island of Rhodes manifest the spirit of cooperation and brotherly love that characterizes worldwide Orthodoxy today.

It was through the untiring efforts of the late Patriarch Athenagoras that several Orthodox Churches joined the World Council of Churches in the last twenty-five years. Furthermore, the Ecumenical Patriarchate has initiated dialogues between the Orthodox on the one hand and the Anglican, the Old Catholic, and the Oriental Churches on the other. The meeting of Patriarch Athenagoras and Pope Paul VI in January 1964 eased the way for a new era in the relations between the Greek Orthodox and the Roman Catholic Church. This was achieved through the efforts of the Ecumenical Patriarchate, which proved an apostle of love, understanding, and cooperation.

Despite its limited resources, the Ecumenical Patriarchate is very active in social and philanthropic projects. It maintains forty philanthropic societies, which minister to the needs of the needy in Istanbul and elsewhere. These societies are under the supervision of the Pneumatike Diakonia, or Spiritual Diaconate. Children are of special concern to this patriarchal organization. It helps poor boys and girls in their tender years and sees them through college. The diaconate grants several scholarships every year and often helps students even during their graduate studies abroad. In addition to offering many scholarships, the Patriarchate supports summer camps for both sexes between the ages of 7 and 14. More than five hundred students benefit from this program annually. There are also camps for working youths, the benefits of which are extended to more than two hundred annually. These are generous numbers when we consider that the faithful of Istanbul number only a few thousands.

The Patriarchate spends several thousands of Turkish liras every month for several poor families in Istanbul and provides many thousands more in dowries for poor girls. The marriage of a poor girl who is under the protection of the Patriarchate takes place in the cathedral of the Patriarchate with a bishop officiating, thus indicating that the mother Church makes no distinction between rich and poor.

The social awareness of the Ecumenical Patriarchate today brings to mind the great philanthropic programs of the same Patriarchate during the Middle Ages, that is, of the Byzantine era. Ecumenical Patriarch Athenagoras I, who was elevated to the patriarchal throne while he was archbishop of North and South America, added new dimensions to the mission of the Patriarchate and was admired for his vision and prophetic charisma.

The Patriarchate of Alexandria is the heir of a rich tradition of theological scholarship and missionary activity. It maintains jurisdiction over all the Greek Orthodox of Egypt and Africa, with a membership of approximately two hundred thousand. Of course, the Church of Alexandria is but a shadow when compared with its past. Nonetheless, in view of its most successful missions in several new African nations, such as Uganda and Tanzania, its vitality should not be underestimated.

The ancient Patriarchate of Jerusalem is an important center of early Christian tradition and faith. It is known as the guardian of the historic sites of the Holy Land, where Jesus was born and taught. Most of its members are of Arabic origin.

The nearby Church of Cyprus is one of the oldest autocephalous Christian communities. It became self-governing during the sixth century, when Justinian granted it special privileges. It has suffered much, from the seventh century up to recent times, as a result of the strategic position of the island and its having been conquered several times. Nevertheless, it has more than half a million members. It is a vigorous Church, with a seminary, three metropolitan episcopates, philanthropic institutions, and periodicals.

The Church of Greece, with a membership of approximately nine million people, was officially recognized as a self-governing church in 1850. She increased both territorially and numerically after a series of revolutionary wars that brought to the Greek nation the territories of Epiros, Thessaly, Macedonia, Thrace, and the Ionian and Aegean islands. Greece is a solidly Orthodox Christian country. The Church is indeed "the soul of Greece," as an American author recently observed.

The Church of Greece is divided into 66 small dioceses, with 7,765 parishes, more or less, whose vitality in the post–World War II period was notable in religious education, social consciousness, and theological scholarship. The catechetical, or Sunday, schools are a source of pride in Greece for both clergymen and laymen. The religious revivals initiated by such movements as Zoe, the Orthodox Christian Unions, Apostolike Diaconia, and Soter, to mention only the most important of them, gave new life to the Church of Greece. During the war and postwar years, between 1940 and 1947, the young people of Greece were sought after by Communist youth organizations and religious youth societies, and most joined one or the other. Young men and women, perplexed and confused as a result of the decadence, injustices, and brutality introduced by the "civilized barbarians" of the twentieth century, desperately needed guidance and structure in their lives.

Several young men I knew would undoubtedly have joined the Communist movement had a vigorous Church and vital religious organizations not attracted them away from communism. The Christian organizations worked through various channels and reached every class of people. The simple peasant as well as the university professor, the young laborer as well as the university student, the parent as well as the young girl, could find in the Church a place of love and solace. The catechetical schools reached their zenith in the middle 1950s. Up to 1954 the Church of Greece counted more than 7,750 well-organized Sunday schools.

As a result of these postwar revivals, Church attendance increased greatly, Bible study became common, participation in the sacraments of confession and Holy Communion became frequent, and the social consciousness of the Church flourished to an unprecedented degree.

Unfortunately, very little is known by the non-Orthodox about the social consciousness of the Greek Orthodox Church. Yet every diocese of Greece is a center of philanthropic activity. Not only has the Church issued encyclicals expressive of her concern for social justice, but each bishop has a treasury of Funds for the Poor and maintains several welfare institutions. Throughout Greece, the Church maintains nearly 2,750 philanthropic institutions including 2,452 funds for daily needs of the poor; 42 orphanages, 123 boarding homes for poor students; 66 homes for the aged; 7 hospitals, and 50 summer camps. The philanthropic work of several dioceses is very impressive. For example, the diocese of Dimitrias, with 124 parishes, maintains twelve charitable institutions. The diocese of Messinia, with a population of perhaps a hundred thousand, supports fourteen philanthropic establishments. The diocese of Lesbos, with 60 parishes, supports twelve welfare institutions.

The concern of the Church is often extended to include dowries for poor or orphaned girls; the distribution of funds to individuals released from prison; the distribution of food and clothing to poor families, schoolchildren, and individuals in want. Many dioceses support impoverished students of theology and other disciplines, including graduate students. Every parish also has a relief treasury, or *logia,* for the needs of the local poor people or needy travelers. However, the social consciousness of the Greek Church is most clearly manifested when disasters strike, such as during the war years and the subsequent foreign occupations, the disastrous earthquakes in the Ionian islands and Thessaly, and other catastrophes. It is no exaggeration to state that the Church has often proved a bastion of social justice and part of the vanguard in welfare and relief programs. During the German occupation of Greece in the 1940s the Church intervened numerous times on behalf of the Jewish people of Greece. Archbishop Damaskinos offered special housing and all the necessary means to save Greek Jews. He made himself and the Greek Church responsible for their future. Damaskinos' endeavors unfortunately failed, but the goodwill and humanism of the Greek Church were manifest.

The social work of the Greek Church was extended to protect and save British and Australian soldiers who were left behind after the German occupation of Greece. No other Church suffered so much from the Axis; she also suffered from the efforts of the Communists to take over Greece during the decade of 1940–1950. More than four hundred clergymen were killed either because they were men of religious principles or because they were patriots. A substantial sacrifice indeed from a church with no more than seven thousand clergymen.

The third aspect that requires special attention is the vitality of theological scholarship in Greek schools of theology today. It is not an exaggeration to state that during the last fifty years Greece has produced great theologians of international reputation. In addition to two schools of theology, the Church supports several seminaries for the training of parish priests. The concern of many theologians is both academic and ecclesiastical.

Greek theology is not only "a theology of the university lecture room." Several works of such theologians and scholars as Panagiotis Trembelas, Ieronymos Kotsonis, Constantine Bonis, Panagiotis Chrestou, Evangelos Theodorou, Constantine Kourkoulas, Basil Moustakis, Elias Mastrogiannopoulos, John Alexiou, John Kolitsaras, Savvas Agourides, Nikos Nissiotis, John Anastasiou, George Mantzarides, Anastasios Giannoulatos, Demetrios Trakatellis, Christos Gianaras, and several more are for educated laymen as well as for academicians and theologians. Some of these theologians are men of university rank and also clergymen. There are several theologians today whose "intrinsic worth is such that any company of modern scholars would gladly and gratefully admit them to their fellowship," as the theologian Frank Gavin once said. If they are little known outside Greece, it is because they write in modern Greek, a language that few Western European and American scholars have come to learn.

Greek Orthodox theology has served often and will continue to serve as a *martyria,* a witness to the theology of the early and the medieval Church; it has contributed significantly to the ecumenical movement through such churchmen as the late archbishop Germanos of Thyateira, the late archbishop Michael, Archbishop Iakovos, Metropolitan Emilianos of Calabria, Archbishop Athenagoras, Professor Hamilcar Alivizatos, and Professor Nikos Nissiotis. Under the aegis of the Ecumenical Patriarchate, Greek Orthodox theology will continue to work for the restoration of the Christian world and the unity of the Church.

The Greek-speaking Orthodox Churches of Constantinople (Istanbul), Alexandria, Jerusalem, Cyprus, and Greece, together with churches of other Orthodox jurisdictions, comprise the Orthodox Church, which was born as a result of the meeting between Jesus Christ, the eternal Logos, and the Greeks in the city of Jerusalem nearly two thousand years ago.

4

Some Aspects
of the Church's
Faith and Experience

A s we indicated in the very beginning of the present work, religion is a complex phenomenon expressed in a variety of ways. Greek Orthodoxy is not an exception. It resembles a polygonal prism, and contains certain aspects that have been either little appreciated or greatly overlooked, such as mysticism and evangelicalism.

Mysticism in the Orthodox Faith

Mysticism cannot be defined, but in broad terms it is the religious experience of the individual who seeks a life of harmony, peace, and continuous communion with the supreme being. Introspection, contemplation, and solitude are prerequisites for the development of an inner religious experience. Constant prayer assures divine intervention, which illuminates the human soul. Divine grace and man's continuous quest assure revelation, or acquisition of divine knowledge. Mysticism is primarily a personal religious experience within the broad framework of the Church. Mysticism tends to stress the individualistic approach of religion.

In one way or another, to some degree, every individual is a mystic. Christian mysticism has its beginning in the teachings of Jesus, Saint Paul, Saint John, and several early Church

Fathers and saints. But mysticism developed into an influential theological stream after the fourth century under the influence of Saint Methodios of Olympos, Makarios of Egypt, John Klimakos, Dionysios the Pseudo-Areopagite, and Maximos the Confessor. All emphasized the need for solitude, meditation, cultivation of the inner life, and continuous communication with the divine. The theological disputes of the fourth and fifth centuries contributed to the cultivation of mysticism, for they convinced certain holy persons that the way to God is inward cultivation. For example, when in the fourth century churchmen argued over the terms *ousia* and *hypostasis* with reference to God, Evagrios of Pontos advised: "In silence let us worship the incomprehensible."

Some Orthodox thinkers have stressed that the exclusive purpose of Christianity is a direct and intuitive experience of God. Among many others Makarios of Egypt views the relationship between God and the individual soul as similar to the intimate relationship between a groom and his bride. The mystical experience is the result of a marriage between the individual soul and Christ. "The soul is wounded by eros or agape for Christ, as a result of which she longs for her consubstantial union with him."

The mystical union is beyond the senses, imagination, or rational explanation. Not all believers can claim such an experience, and the Church acknowledges that God has bestowed different gifts on different people. There is no need to doubt the existence of such religious experiences. If we accept that the human soul is of God, created by Him in His own image and likeness, it is not difficult to understand that the human soul longs for God and finds no contentment, peace, joy, or certainty apart from Him.

The human soul lives in the divine reality even though this reality transcends the soul and the world and at the same time is in the soul and in the world. The human person lives in God but is not absorbed in or dictated by God. The relationship between the two is one of love. The human intellect and will become subordinate to God's love and will. The creator loves His creature, and the creature is continuously drawn to its creator. The prevailing theme in Orthodox mystical theology is the love affair between God and His creatures, who meet in the person of the God-man, Christ.

God manifests His love throughout His creation as the creator, the redeemer, and the restorer. By grace a person can imitate God, however imperfectly, as restorer and reformer of the human social order and of the condition of all humanity in general.

The emphasis on the love that God communicates to people and the divine experience to which they are invited reveals the ethos of Greek Christianity, which is not so much psychological security, freedom from fear, or even doctrinal guidance, but communion with God. The doctrine that man is made in the likeness of God leads to the doctrine of the deification of man. Thus to imitate God's love, or *philanthropia,* is "to practice being God," as Clement of Alexandria formulated it. The imitator of God's *philanthropia* lives the very life of God. Orthodox spirituality, as expressed in several liturgical services, teaches that God is not distant, abstract, remote, or unapproachable, but that He is the Father whose name is *Philanthropos* and whose nature is *philanthropia;* that is, God's name and nature are love. "And the more one loves God, the more one enters within God," as Clement of Alexandria writes.

The soul's imitation of God's love is not an ordinary stirring or movement of the soul but a divine gift, made in response to its longings, to its faith and desire. The gift is a "divine energy," which induces a fire in the soul and wins it to God's love and will.

The eleventh-century mystic Saint Symeon calls God "Holy Love" in one of his homilies:

> O Holy Love, he who does not know you has never tasted the sweetness of your mercies which only living experience can give us. But he who has known you, or who has been known by you, can never again have even the smallest doubt. For you are the fulfillment of the law, and you fill, burn, enkindle, embrace my heart with measureless charity. You are the teacher of the prophets, the faithful friend of the apostles, the strength of the martyrs, the inspiration of fathers and doctors, the perfecting of all the saints. And you, O Love, prepare even me for the true service of God.

The true lover of God is also a genuine lover of persons. Elsewhere Symeon writes of love as the crown of all other virtues, such as humility, penitence, and faith. Love enables the soul to know the purpose of its divinity and its destiny upon earth. The fulfillment of human life is to love, and through the experience of love the soul is united with God. Symeon cries out in praise of love: "O blessed bond, O indescribable strength, O heavenly disposition, how excellent is the soul which is animated by the divine inspiration and perfected in exceeding love of God and man."

Similar views were developed later by Nicholas Kabasilas. In his famous *Commentary on the Divine Liturgy*, Kabasilas called upon man to offer doxologies to God's exceeding and unfathomable love for man, out of which He emptied himself of His supernatural exaltation, assuming human flesh in order to walk among His adopted brethren and draw them back to the eternal God.

Because God's presence in the world is an existential reality, with concrete illustrations of His concern for the cosmos and human beings in particular, they ought to reciprocate and express their love for God with love for their fellow human beings. Orthodox theology takes very seriously the Biblical verses: "If any one says, 'I love God,' and hates his brother, he is a liar; for he who does not love his brother whom he has seen, cannot love God whom he has not seen. And this commandment we have from him, that he who loves God should love his brother also" (1 Jn. 4:20–21).

The concept of a vertically and horizontally understood *philanthropia* is important for our age and relevant for any epoch. Because of God's example, the whole human family becomes an object of concern for all believers. The dialogue of love escapes the realm of sentimental yearning and transforms itself into a reality. On the basis of the same reasoning, Christ, who manifested the Father's as well as His own *agape*, is acknowledged as the cosmic redeemer, drawing to himself all people who display a genuine concern for the destiny of the human family.

It is certain that the apophatic element dominates liturgical and patristic theology. God and the divine are beyond human ability to comprehend. We know that God is "he that is," and "infinite and incomprehensible," to use the classic words of Saint John Damascene. Nevertheless, God manifests His energies, including *philanthropia*, which is the crown of them all and ecumenical in character: it leads to the final restoration of justice, the salvation of human beings, and the realization of God's desire for their participation in God's eternal life.

Philanthropos or *Christos Eleemon* or *Christos Evergetes*—here is revealed the ideal Christ, whose deep concern over humanity Christians must imitate in their daily lives. Believers in and imitators of the *philanthropia* of God are no longer individualists living by and for themselves; they become their "brothers' keepers." The theme of God's search and love for man is diffused throughout the Divine Liturgy and the other sacraments of the Church. On the one hand there is the holiness and transcendence, the awe and mystery, the "metaphysical" wonder, of God and on the other hand there is the realized immanence and presence, the "unfathomable *philanthropia*" of God. It is because of His mercy, love, and compassion that God condescends to walk among us in order to raise us to godhood. "Lord have mercy upon us, you who suffered for us to free us from our iniquities, you who humbled yourself in order to raise us," as the congregation sings in one of the Church's hymns.

In the liturgy we glorify God's great mercy. It is because of God's constant manifestation of philanthropy that the weakling becomes mighty, the carnal becomes spiritual, and the spiritual sees the glory of the fountainhead from which the soul derives strength, courage, and achievement.

Greek Orthodoxy views God as Being, as personal, individual, and distinct from nature and man, but also as the being in whom all other beings participate and in whom all existence moves. People apprehend God as immediately as their own existence and come to know Him fully through their interactions and relationships with their fellow human beings.

The concept of *Theos Philanthropos* implies a special understanding of history. One sees the continuity of creation from the event of cosmogony to the resurrection of life after Christ's victory over death. The *philanthropia* of God brought the world into being before time was, it was manifested in the historical person of Christ, and it is perpetuated in the work of the Holy Spirit. Therefore all events and all history are dominated by God's love in action, permanent, constant, and developing.

In Orthodoxy there is only "sacred" history, not because there is no "secular" history but because the two are inseparable. Many historical events belong to both. To be sure there was the "sacred" history of ancient Israel, but God disclosed himself through "secular," or natural, history as well. Even the "sacred" history of Israel was not totally "sacred," for it was developed in the context of "secular" history. As sacred history was conditioned by secular history, the latter too was conditioned by sacred history.

The incarnation of the Messiah-Logos was the fulfillment of sacred history, and was accomplished in the context of Greco-Roman history—the Greek cultural and intellectual milieu and the umbrella of the Roman state. History is called "sacred" because God is in history, revealing himself in and through history, whether by the prophets or by the philosophers, the Israelites or the Gentiles.

Orthodox worship stresses the infinite love of God in the Trinity, God the Father who creates, God the Son who redeems, and God the Holy Spirit who sanctifies, gives life, and leads to a final recapitulation of God's redemptive process. His people, the Church, should emulate God's love. As the bride of a loving bridegroom, the Church must pursue a dialogue of love among her members and with those outside her jurisdiction. Because of God's *philanthropia*, there is hope that through the grace of God people can come together as adopted children under the fatherhood of God.

The Evangelicalism of the Church

Many factors have influenced the formation of dogma and the evolution of Orthodox theology. The *evangelion*, or gospel, has contributed the most. Holy Scripture is the fountain and essence of Greek Orthodox theology; all other elements are auxiliary. The very substance of the creed, ethos, and worship of Orthodoxy derives from the *evangelion*. But writers, either of the Orthodox Church or of other persuasions, have neglected the evangelical, or Biblical, character of Orthodoxy—its faith, ethics, worship, and culture. Even in serious manuals this facet of the Orthodox Church goes almost unheeded.

Some theologians have stressed that the Orthodox Church is the guardian of the most genuine apostolic tradition and that she is the Church of the early ecumenical decrees. Others have emphasized that she is a patristic Church, or that the Church is freedom fused with authority and the weight of the past. These and other characteristics—apostolicity, catholicity, traditionalism, moderation, unbroken continuity—have been described in several manuals, but rarely the evangelical.

Because of this lacuna in Orthodox textbooks from the early nineteenth century to the present, many Western theologians and ordinary faithful have seen the Orthodox as Biblically illiterate, if not superstitious and paganistic. Because the outward appearance of Orthodoxy is liturgical and sacramental, many Western Christians have regarded Orthodox liturgy and sacramental life as antagonistic to Holy Scripture. Even now, Orthodoxy is considered extensively involved in symbolism and ritual.

What follows is a brief attempt to turn the polygonal prism of Orthodoxy to another of its several facets, one which has ecumenical dimensions, since the Biblical nature of the Orthodox Church furnishes a common ground in the dialogues that take place between the Orthodox and the Roman Catholic as well as Protestant churches. In fact, Orthodox theology in nearly every one of its ramifications is evangelical rather than patristic, philosophical, or liturgical. What has been characterized as sacramental, liturgical, patristic, or intellectual has Biblical roots. Of course, Biblical theology is sufficiently broad to be, at the same time, liturgical and sacramental. The words and symbols of the liturgy, the mysteries (or sacraments), and other rites are derived from the Bible. Bible and dogma, Bible and ethical precepts, Bible and liturgical services and prayers—all are fused in Orthodox theology.

The Biblical character of the Greek Orthodox Church is not difficult to discover. Ecclesiastical writers throughout the history of the Church have never ceased to recommend the reading of the Scriptures. The Bible has never been the exclusive book of the clergy or the monks. Saint John Chrysostom prepared the way. In an appeal to the laity for Bible study Chrysostom writes: "Your mistake is in believing that the reading of the Scriptures concerns only monks . . . for you it is still more necessary since you are in the midst of the world. There is something worse than not reading the Scriptures, and that is to believe that this reading is useless . . . a satanic practice."

The Divine Liturgy itself is not only mystery or eucharistic doxology. It is also a liturgy of the Word of God, since the first part of the service includes two readings from the New Testament and a homily, which is usually an exegesis of one of the two readings. When one reads or listens to the Word of God one becomes a *theodidaktos*, or one taught by God, as Clement of Alexandria writes.

Because of the central position accorded to the *evangelion*, the Orthodox Church is an evangelical church par excellence. Orthodox piety and spirituality, sacramental mysticism, and patristic theology are based on the belief of the living presence of Christ not only in the Eucharist but also in the gospels, which constitute the record of Christ's teaching. God's manifestation in history, God's revelation in the earthly life of Christ, His work through the Apostles, His presence in the history of the Church—all constitute a living reality unfolded in the prayer life of the Church and involving each of the faithful. The Bible is viewed not simply as antiquarian "history" but as "holy history," which manifests the acts of God in the past, lives on into the present, and forms a guidepost for the future.

While the Greek cultural and intellectual tradition played a paramount role in the life of the Church, the inner strength and real source of Orthodox theology must be sought in the Bible. During the medieval Greek era, the Church felt a special pride in being the custodian and teacher of the Scriptures while at the same time taking great care to preserve the Greek literary and cultural heritage. Despite the Platonic idealism and the substratum of Aristotelian philosophical tradition and scholastic categories in patristic thought, love for the simple teachings of Christ dominates the writings of many Fathers and theologians. Orthodoxy in general was illuminated and modified by the light of Biblical revelation. As Lev Gillet has put it: "Orthodoxy presents a [Greek] classical landscape bathed in the light of the Logos."

The Bible is both a divine and a human record—it is a theanthropic document, infallible and fallible, an eternal and a temporal record. In the Bible God reveals Himself either through prophets, kings, and shepherds or through His own Son. In the Bible man seeks to "discover and touch" God (Acts 17:27). This encounter, however, between the heavenly Father and earthly son or daughter is primarily a revelation and self-disclosure of God because man is still an infant or even still unborn spiritually. What the community of believers needed to record about the life of Christ, as well as its own life and practical needs, was designated Holy Scripture. This recorded revelation stands or falls by the testimony and the authority of the Church. The testimony, or *martyria,* of the Church to the authority of the written revelation is an absolute necessity.

The recorded revelation was the work of people living within the community of believers and speaking primarily to other believers for their edification. The Ecclesia is the guardian (the *thematophylax*) of all God's manifestations to human beings, including, of course, the recorded activity of God's self-disclosure. Church and Bible are inseparably united in a harmonious and mutually supportive entity. As the repository of revelation, as the recorder of God's manifestation (*phanerosis*) and God's involvement in history, the Church is by nature Biblical, for she has the Bible in her bosom and is the official interpreter of the Bible. It follows that the theology, the teaching, the commandments, and the ethos of the Church are Biblical.

As the Church is Biblical in her essence, likewise the central theme of the Bible is the Church, the Church as a holy organism born before all ages, reconstituted or revitalized in time and in space by God's Logos. That is, the Bible speaks of the Church as the living body of Christ and as the Christ perpetuated throughout the ages.

The reading of the Bible is a living tradition. It is a constant part of all major services: vespers and matins, liturgies and sacraments, sacramental services—such as the blessing of the waters—and all other brief services. Almost the whole New

Testament and much of the Old Testament is read throughout the Church year in Church worship. The Bible occupies a central place of honor in every Orthodox home.

But in addition to the specific pericopes from the Old or the New Testament read in each service, each service is imbued with Scriptural verses and elements. Each prayer and hymn of every liturgy, sacrament, or service refers to some Biblical event; the number and extent of the scriptural elements varies from service to service.

The Psalms, Genesis, and the book of Isaiah enjoy more popularity than the other Old Testament books. Exodus and the Wisdom of Solomon follow. From the New Testament, Matthew, Luke, 1 Corinthians, Romans, the Gospel of John, and Hebrews, in that order, are the most popular.

A recent study of the Liturgies of the Presanctified Gifts, Saint Basil, and Saint John Chrysostom, as well as of the sacraments of baptism, chrism, holy unction, and matrimony, compiled by this writer, reveals a very clear dependence by these services upon the Bible. Approximately 25 percent of these services consists of direct Biblical borrowings. The material in the services that alludes to or is inspired by Scripture is even greater.

The Liturgy of the Presanctified Gifts includes sixty-one verses and elements from both the Old and the New Testament. The extensive use of Psalms bears witness to the antiquity of the liturgy and its soteriological message. The Liturgy of Saint John Chrysostom has absorbed 237 verses, of which 124 are from the Old Testament and 113 from the New Testament. The prayers of Saint Basil's Liturgy, which are not found in that of Chrysostom, include 205 Scriptural verses and elements, 68 of which are from the Old Testament and 137 from the New Testament.

Here are three prayers illustrative of the Biblical character of Orthodox liturgical prayer:

> 1) The First Prayer of the Faithful (Liturgy of St. Basil)
>   It is you, O Lord, who have shown us this *great mystery* [1 Tim. 3:16] of salvation; it is you who have deemed us, your humble and unworthy servants, worthy of the service of your holy Altar. *Through the power of your Holy Spirit, make*

us then able to fulfill this holy office [Rom. 15:13; 2 Cor. 3:6; 2 Cor. 4:1], so that, *standing* without condemnation *before your holy glory* [Jude 24; Song of the Three Young Men 31], we may offer you *a sacrifice of praise* [Heb. 13:15], for it is you *who work all things in all* [1 Cor. 12:6]. Grant us, O Lord, that our offering for our sins *and for the unawareness of the people* [Heb. 9:7] may *be acceptable and pleasing to you* [Phil. 4:18].

2) Prayer of the Anaphora (Liturgy of St. Basil)

O You who are Being, *Master* and *Lord* [Jer. 1:6], God almighty and adorable Father: *it is truly fitting* [2 Thess. 1:3] and right and worthy of *the immensity of your holiness* [Ps. 145:5] that we *praise you* [Ps. 65:1], sing to you, bless you, adore you, give thanks to you, glorify you *who alone are truly God* [Jn. 5:44]; that we offer you a *spiritual worship with a repentant heart and a humble spirit* [Rom. 12:1; Song of the Three Young Men 16; Ps. 51:17], for it is you who granted us *the favor of knowing your truth* [Heb. 10:26]. *How could anyone tell your might and sing the praises you deserve, or describe all your marvels in all places and times?* [Ps. 106:2; Ps. 26:7; Job 5:9]. *O Master of All, Lord of heaven and earth and of all creatures visible and invisible, who are enthroned upon a seat of glory, who plumb the depths* [Mt. 11:25; 3 Mac. 2:2; Wis. 9:10; Song of the Three Young Men 32], who are eternal, invisible, beyond comprehension and description and change, *the Father of our Lord Jesus Christ the great God and Savior, the object of our hope!* [2 Cor. 1:3; Tit. 2:13; 1 Tim. 1:1]. *For He is the image of your goodness, the seal bearing your perfect likeness, revealing You his Father through Himself; He is the living word, the true God, the Wisdom from before all ages, the Life, the sanctification, the Power, the true light* [Wis. 7:26; Heb. 1:3; Jn. 14:9; 1 Jn. 5:20; 1 Cor. 1:30; Ps. 54:19 LXX; Jn. 14:6; 1 Cor. 1:24]. By Him the Holy Spirit was made manifest, *the Spirit of Truth, the Gift of adoption, the foretaste of the future inheritance, the first fruits of eternal good* [Jn. 14:17; Rom. 8:15; Eph. 1:14; Rom. 8:23], the life-giving power, the fountain of sanctification. Empowered by Him, every rational and intelligent creature sings eternally to your glory, *for all are your servants* [Ps. 119:91]. It is you the *angels*, archangels, *thrones and dominions, the principalities* and the virtues, *the powers* and the cherubim of many eyes adore; it is you the *seraphim surround, one with six wings and the other with six wings; and with two wings they cover their faces, and with two their feet, and with two they fly, and they cry one to the other* [1 Pet.

3:22; Col. 1:16; Is. 6:2–3] with tireless voice and perpetual praise.

3) First Prayer of the Faithful (Liturgy of St. John Chrysostom)

We thank you, Lord God of Hosts [Rev. 11:17; Ps. 84:8], for having made us worthy to stand at this moment before your holy altar, and throw ourselves on your mercies for our sins and *the faults of the people* [Heb. 9:7]. Accept, O God, our entreaty; make us worthy *to offer you prayers and supplications* [Heb. 5:7] and unbloody sacrifices for all your people; and *by the power of* your Holy *Spirit* [Lk. 4:14; 2 Cor. 3:6] strengthen us whom you have *appointed to this your ministry* [1 Tim. 1:12]: *so that at all times and places* [Wis. 19:22], without blame or offence, *with the testimony of a clear conscience, we may call upon you* [2 Cor. 1:12; 1 Cor. 1:2]; and that *hearing* us you may *have mercy on us in the plenitude of your goodness* [1 Kings 8:34; Ps. 69:13].

Among the sacraments, baptism's Scriptural nature reveals how the early Church understood the soteriological problem, the nature of man, and the meaning of his redemption. The service includes 186 Biblical verses. The Old Testament is represented by 94 verses, the new Testament by 92.

Despite the brevity of the sacrament of Chrism, it too is saturated with Biblical material. It includes 30 verses, 17 of which are from the New Testament and the remaining 13 from the Old Testament.

An examination of the Scriptural structure of holy unction, apart from its seven Gospel and Epistle readings, reveals the healing attributes bestowed upon the Church and the therapeutic mission that is expected of her. In the sacrament of holy unction Christ works as physician to the human soul and body. The lections of the sacrament deal primarily with human suffering or spiritual affliction and reveal God's mercy, love, and intervention on mankind's behalf. Like Christ, the Church must be concerned with human suffering. There are 196 Scriptural verses from both Testaments in this rite. The Old Testament leads with 109, against 87 from the New Testament.

The Biblical material in the sacrament of matrimony, apart from the two standard pericopes, consists of 130 verses. The use of the Old Testament prevails, with 90 verses against 40 for the New Testament. In addition there are numerous allusions and references to Biblical personalities such as Isaac, Sarah, and Joseph. In the Biblical material of this sacrament the emphasis of the Church is on the sanctity of the conjugal relationship, with special reference to the couple's procreative task and the call to spiritual perfection. It also manifests the Church's strong opposition to separation and divorce. The unity of husband and wife is like the union between Christ and His Church.

The hymns of the Church are full of direct or indirect Scriptural references, synonyms, and concepts, to a greater degree than are the Church services and prose prayers. This is confirmed by a study of the Easter Canon hymn of Saint John of Damascus, the Christmas Canon of Cosmas of Maiuma, and the Akathistos Hymn of Romanos the Melodist. Of 807 lines of hymns, 369 lines include concepts and ideas taken directly from the New Testament. In other words, about 45 percent of the hymns consist of Biblical material. Breaking down the lines into words and terms, excluding articles and conjunctions, we discover that of 2,219 words from the hymns mentioned above, 783 are taken from the New Testament, some 35 percent. And a recent study of the great Canon of Saint Andrew of Crete, which includes 250 hymns (*troparia*), revealed that Saint Andrew's masterpiece is filled with Biblical passages and allusions. One hundred ninety-three *troparia* include Scriptural material. The author of this third study concludes that 77 percent of the Canon's material is Biblical.

In addition to the liturgical use of the Bible in Church liturgy and hymnology, the study of the Scriptures has always been encouraged in the Orthodox Church. In countries where Orthodoxy predominates, even the illiterate have learned by heart whole psalms and other portions of the Scriptures. In the early and medieval Church there were persons who knew many parts of the Bible by heart, and candidates for the priesthood were required before ordination to learn a certain number of psalms, plus a gospel and several epistles. But today this is not a practical requirement for service in the Church, though Scriptural sayings and phrases, like proverbs and mottos, come readily in the speech of both clergymen and laity.

The Scriptures were diligently studied by monastic communities, whether they were composed of intellectuals or simple monks. In practically every monastic ordinance, or *typikon*, there are strong recommendations for the study of the Bible, not as a literary document but as a guide for everyday living. "Study of the holy scriptures, spiritual exercise, prudence, and obedience" were virtues to be pursued by all monks, as monastic rules and the biographies of great saints proclaim. Such canons are even inscribed on the icons of various saints, such as Euthymios and Symeon.

The Church Fathers and theologians have always encouraged Bible study. It has been estimated that if all the Scriptural quotations in John Chrysostom's works were put together, the whole Bible could be constructed. Chrysostom advocated the study of the Scriptures by clergymen and all believers alike. He advised: "Let us give diligent heed to the study of the Scriptures; the study of the Bible expels despondency, engenders pleasure, extirpates vice, makes virtue take root. In the tumult of life Bible study will save you from suffering like those who are tossed by troubled waves. While the sea of life rages, you sail on with calm weather because the study of the Scriptures serves you as a pilot."

Many Church Fathers accorded absolute authority to the Scriptures. For them the revelation of God in its dual form, oral and written, was deposited in the Church. On the one hand was the continuous tradition of the Church and on the other the Holy Scriptures. Holy tradition and Holy Scriptures were viewed as two sides of the same coin. The apostolic tradition stood at the root of both.

From as early as the second century, ecclesiastical writers viewed the Bible as the source of Christian doctrine. Origen was a pronounced biblicist. His writings abound in Scriptural elements and appeal over and over again to Holy Scripture as the ultimate criterion of faith. Saint Athanasios proclaimed that "the holy and inspired Scriptures are fully sufficient for the proclamation of the truth." Cyril of Jerusalem was even more emphatic. He wrote: "With regard to the divine and saving mysteries of faith no doctrine, however trivial, may be taught without the backing of the divine Scriptures. . . . For our saving faith derives its force, not from capricious reasonings, but from what may be proved out of the Bible." John Chrysostom and many other Fathers dwell at length on the absolute authority of the Bible regarding doctrinal norms. For them, of course, the Bible was simply written tradition. Cyril of Jerusalem emphasized the apostolicity of abiding by the unwritten as well as the written tradition. In the Christological controversies, the ultimate appeal of Theodoretos of Cyrrhos was to the teaching of the Fathers, who derived their wisdom and inspiration from the "Divine Fountain," from the divinely inspired Scripture as a whole.

Because much of the theological effort of the Fathers was spent on the exposition of the Bible, and because their writings as a whole are impregnated with Biblical material, it may be inferred that patristic theology is actually Biblical theology. Many doctrines that they supported had first to be established on a Biblical basis. It is not irrelevant to observe here that even the Orthodox sermon as a whole is biblically oriented. To be sure, Orthodox priests and lay preachers are free to select their subject matter from various sources, such as liturgical writings, patristic texts, lives of the saints, or current national and social issues. Nevertheless, the average Orthodox preacher turns to his Bible for inspiration and for his theme. Both in theory and in practice the Holy Scriptures constitute the most important source for a homily, or kerygma.

Thus dogmatic and ethical, patristic and liturgical theology in the Orthodox Church have Biblical foundations and Scriptural content. Holy Scripture, which has saturated the liturgical and prayer life of the Church, her hymnology and hagiography, and all the other aspects of her intellectual and moral life, occupies a central place in Orthodox theology today. Modern Orthodox theologians see the Bible as the ultimate criterion of theological truth, whose authority has been and remains "unlimited" and "self-sufficient." Neither doctrine nor liturgy can serve as substitute for the word of God.

But the Biblical character of the Church should not be viewed separately from its traditional side. The latter is a strong characteristic and of equal importance. Sacred tradition is not an accumulation of human sayings that have been transmitted to us. It is rather the life of the Church under the constant guidance of the Holy Spirit; it is the handiwork of the Holy Spirit in the life and the thought of the Church; it is the revelation of the Holy Spirit incorporated in the doctrinal life of the Church; it is the faith to which the Church synods and Fathers bear witness and of which the Orthodox Church is the vigilant and abiding custodian. This is in perfect agreement with the promise of Christ. He said to His disciples: "When the Spirit of truth comes, he will guide you into all the truth; for he will not speak on his own authority, but whatever he hears he will speak, and he will declare to you the things that are to come" (Jn. 16:13). Because of her confidence in and attachment to the person of the Holy Spirit, the Orthodox Church has remained pneumatological.

Sacred icons, the cross, candles, and the like in an Orthodox house of worship are not elements of sacred tradition, which deals with doctrine and faith; rather they constitute a heritage of pious tradition. They are only symbols intended to help in the religious instruction of the faithful. They correspond to the needs of the human senses and are in no way idolatrous. Icons remind the faithful of the reality of the divine. A distinction should be made between tradition and sacred tradition. The former is human and the latter is divine. There is much ritualism and symbolism in the worship of the Orthodox Church, perhaps too much in the eyes of many Orthodox Christians. Of course a great deal of it can be traced back to Old Testament times, while a portion derives from the religious tradition of antiquity. For example, incense is used in the Church because the believers ask God to accept their prayers "as incense before" him (Ps. 141:2). The faithful make the sign of the cross to remind themselves that the Son of God was crucified for their salvation. The outward symbol of the cross is the expression of an inner conversation with God. These elements constitute an educational religious tradition.

Icons of Jesus Christ, His Mother, the patriarchs of the Old Testament, the Apostles, the saints, and the martyrs are found in Orthodox houses of worship and most Orthodox homes. They are used to emphasize the living reality of the sacred persons depicted on them. There is in the Orthodox Church a strong feeling of the reality of the supernatural. There is no death, only life, whether upon the earth or beyond it. Thus the celestial beings are united with humanity in the bosom of the Ecclesia, which transcends both time and space. "The earth is the Lord's and the fullness thereof, the world and those who dwell therein"(Ps. 24:1). All things were made for the service and instruction of man. There is nothing pagan in symbolism as long as it remains a means and not an end in itself.

Abuses can and do happen in every sphere of life. It is possible for a Christian to make an icon the object of worship. It is equally possible for someone to abuse the meaning and the significance of the Holy Scriptures and become a bibliolater. Man lives by symbols and ritual whether he realizes it or not. As long as these remain means to virtue and piety there is nothing alarming about them. Icons and symbols express much that words cannot, and their use in a limited mesure is not only permissible but desirable for the human heart and mind. They evoke feeling rather than cold logic, a natural part of life rather than an academic or formal aspect, a source of inspiration and instruction.

It is important to note here that though the Church allows the depiction of Christ in His human form, she never permits the separation of the divine from the human element. Thus an icon of Christ is always an icon of Christ the God-man. Likewise the icons of Theotokos, the saints, the angels, and other figures of the invisible Church are not realistic representations but depictions and projections of the virtues and saintliness of the personalities involved, presented to mortals for emulation.

In brief, the Orthodox Church appeals to divine revelation as incorporated in the Holy Scriptures and sacred tradition and realizes an unbroken continuity with the original Church, not only in her faith and sacramental and prayer life, but also in her culture and administration.

Although the Orthodox Church believes and claims that she is the true Church, she is neither intolerant nor isolated. In fact, she willingly listens to the views of others. Despite her adamant position in matters of faith, she participates in such organizations as the National Council of Churches in the

United States and the World Council of Churches. While very few, if any, Protestant or Roman Catholic clergymen or theologians study in Greek Orthodox theological schools, many Orthodox clergy and theologians study in Protestant or Roman Catholic theological institutions with the approval of their superiors. The Orthodox Church works and prays for the integration of all Christians in faith, in love, and in hope within the true Church, which is Christ on earth perpetuated until His second coming and the last judgment. She prays constantly "for the peace of the whole world, for the stability of the Holy Churches of God, and for the union of all." Indeed as Dr. James K. McCord, President of Princeton Theological Seminary, writes: "The Greek Orthodox Church is one of the pioneering bodies and the call to unity of the ecumenical Patriarch is one of the milestones in ecumenical history."

She has entered into the ecumenical movement and participates in dialogues in order to bear witness to the ancient unadulterated faith in a confident, fraternal manner. She is confident because she has remained faithful to the historical, theological, ethical, and cultural ideas of early Christianity.

The Orthodox Church is one of the most democratic of Christian Churches. With very rare exceptions her clergy are ordained with the approval of the laity. Laymen play an important role in the administration of the Church. They are elected to the executive council of the Church, and they have great administrative responsibilities in the local parish. All may occupy a significant position and work for the well-being of the body of the Church.

The Greek Orthodox Church preserves the ancient system of administration known as synodic; it is not an absolutist one, but neither is it loose enough to produce anarchy and extreme individualism. An examination of her administration will illustrate her system of freedom and discipline. A deacon serves a presbyter in a parish or a bishop in his diocese. A presbyter, or priest, is the center of spiritual authority over his parish, receiving his authority from the bishop. And the bishop is the head of the Church in a given district or diocese. But over the local bishop stands the synod, or the totality of bishops. Jesus Christ is the head of the synod and the Church as a whole.

The Patristic and Monastic Aspects of the Church

The Greek Orthodox Church is also a patristic Church, that is, a Church which honors many Fathers and saints. One cannot fail to observe that Orthodox Christians show devotion to and speak with reverence about the numerous saints and Fathers of the Church. The memory of one saint or—a rare example—as many as two thousand saints is observed on one single day, and several Sundays of the ecclesiastical year are put aside for a certain group of Church Fathers, such as the Fathers of the first ecumenical synod, those of the second, or of the seventh. Patriarchs and personalities of the Old Testament, as well as saints and disciples of New Testament times and of the long history of Christianity are invoked in every service of the Orthodox Church, as expressed in the following prayer from the service of Orthros:

> O God, save your people, and bless your inheritance; visit your world with mercies and bounties. Exalt the estate of Orthodox Christians, and bestow upon us your rich blessings. We ask all these through the intercession of our all-holy Theotokos and ever-virgin Mary; by the might of the precious and life-giving cross; by the protection of the honorable heavenly angelic powers; at the supplications of the honorable, glorious prophet, forerunner and baptist John; of the holy, glorious and all-laudable apostles; of all the Fathers among the saints, the great hierarchs and ecumenical teachers . . . of the holy, glorious and victorious martyrs; of our venerable and God-bearing Fathers; of the holy and righteous ancestors of God Jesus, Joachim and Anna; of Saint [or saints] . . . whose memory we celebrate, and of all your saints, we beseech you . . . have mercy upon us.

During the offertory service, or *prothesis*, the priest commemorates many Old Testament personages, such as Moses, Aaron, Elijah, Elisha, David, and Daniel. The chosen people of the world before Christ and after Him are commemorated and united in the bosom of the Church along with the angels.

But why is so much emphasis laid on the saints and Church Fathers? The answer is closely related to the Orthodox conception of the nature of the Church. The saints and the Fathers constitute her conscience, because as witnesses to the living flame of the Holy Spirit they experienced the presence of Christ in their lives and bore witness to it before the world. The blood they shed for the faith, the oral and the written word they proclaimed, the hymns and the services they wrote, make up the life of the Church.

The Orthodox believe that the saints and holy men are always present in the faith and life of their Church. They are the perpetual teachers of the gospel and the supreme embodiments of the life of Christ. As heralds of the Holy Spirit, the Fathers purified the faith from heretical influences and defined all the major doctrines of Christianity, such as the Holy Trinity, the natures of Christ, the person of the Holy Spirit, the nature of the Church, and the function of her sacraments. They became "the golden mouths of the Logos . . . the sweet-smelling flowers of Paradise, illuminating stars of the world and the glory of mankind," as one of the many Orthodox hymns declaims.

Among the many saints, martyrs, and Fathers honored in the Greek Orthodox Church from Saint Stephen the first martyr to Saint Chrysostom, bishop of Smyrna in the 1920s, the most popular have been Saints Polycarp, Ignatios, Anthony, Athanasios, Basil the Great, Gregory of Nazianzos, John Chrysostom, George, Demetrios, Theodore, Eustathios, Maximos the Confessor, John of Damascus, Photios, Philaretos Eleemon, Gregory Palamas, George the New Martyr, Nikodemos the Hagiorite, and Nektarios of Salamis. Some of these saints were simple folk, others were theologians and clergymen, still others were wise men and scholars. There were even kings and socially prominent people, who considered the comforts of this world not worth comparing with the glory that is to be revealed (cf. Rom. 8:18).

There are faithful in the Orthodox Church, both lay and clergy, who renounce the everyday concerns of life—marriage, family, and profession—in order to devote their lives to prayer and contemplation. We call such a person a *monachos* (monk). What is a monk? Theodore Studites writes that "a monk is a man who looks only toward God, who is drawn to God and is close to God, desiring to serve only God, being in peace with God and becoming an instrument of peace with other human beings."

Monasticism was born not only out of the individual's desire to live a perfect religious life but also as a reaction to the secularism that infiltrated the Church as early as the third century of the Christian Era. Monasticism flourished in the Christian East and assumed various forms and characteristics. There were monks who adopted a life of solitude, while others joined monastic communities, devoting themselves to a number of activities—painting, manufacturing religious articles, or serving their fellowmen as medical aides, teachers, or physicians.

But monasticism declined after the nineteenth century, and today there are not many monastic communities either in Greece or in other countries where Orthodoxy prevails. Mount Athos, with its several monastic communities, is the most important and the most famous. Altogether there may be no more than 5,000 monks in the Greek-speaking Orthodox Church. Commenting on the life and character of the monks on Mount Athos, Professor Frederic Will, in an article in the *Yale Review* a few years ago, writes:

> Their lives are whole, prayer and painting are parts of a single devotional existence. The joy is clear enough on their faces. The monks are imaginative, delicate people with a great devotion to their work. Some of them seemed to me among the most broadly human . . . . I was astonished, partly, simply at the existence of such a place . . . . The wholeness of the artistic lives led there is exemplary. Their art and joy seemed to have found one another.

The Relevance of the Church Today

Orthodoxy can contribute her own light to modern man, for she is, indeed, very relevant to our times. She stands on the optimistic side of the different conflicting ideologies and creeds of the twentieth century. Western Christendom suffers from a number of dilemmas, such as the opposition of nature and grace, faith and works, the oral word and the sacrament, Scripture and tradition, the clergy and the laity, and other theological problems. The Orthodox Church has no such dilemmas. She emphasizes a natural revelation in harmony with revealed grace, faith and good works, the word and the sacrament, Bible and tradition, clergy and laity. Divine revelation is viewed not as sudden lightning or a thunderbolt from the sky, but as a cosmic sun whose rays converge in the person of Christ and continuing under the guidance of the Holy Spirit. The Orthodox believe in a revelation whose rays have penetrated many minds and thoughts through various channels in the course of man's history. Orthodoxy is optimistic because of its belief in the dignity of man; because of its doctrine of the deification of human nature under God; because of its belief in the *philanthropia* of God and of man. The gospel of the Orthodox Ecclesia is the gospel of the resurrection, of triumph, and of victory. For in Orthodoxy the human being does not stand alone. Greek Orthodoxy believes that there is only holy history: That God reigns supreme and all evolves under His watchful providence and plans.

The significance that Orthodoxy places on humanity can be considered its unique contribution to modern thought. To the Orthodox Church, a person is much more than a biological being, a social animal, or a sexual phenomenon. He or she is a created dependent being, made by God, a psychosomatic entity, a being made of dust and deity, made "a little less than God" (Ps. 8:5) and at the same time "like the beasts that perish" (Ps. 49:12). The Church teaches that the power that should regulate the lives of men is an expression of *philanthropia*— agape, a unique contribution the Orthodox Church can make to the modern world, for it is the answer to the agony and spiritual isolation of modern man.

The Orthodox Church emphasizes brotherly love not only toward her members and toward Christians of other faiths, but toward all men. It is a fundamental doctrine of the Orthodox faith that all men created in the image of God are equal; for God there is no inequality between colored and white, male and female, one nationality or race and another. Christ restored this human image, which had been almost destroyed because of man's rebellion against God. All men are called to the restoration accomplished by the resurrection of Christ.

Of course, the ancient Greeks' concept of man has much in common with the Christian view. For the Phythagorean philosophers the spirit of man was simply a fallen deity imprisoned in the human body. And for the Stoic philosophers the soul of man was a spark of divinity that upon death of the body returns to the universal God. But while in Greek antiquity the divine element within us is assimilated by the universal deity upon death, in the view of Christianity man preserves his individuality by the grace of God. Man is not only the supreme being upon the earth, but an immortal being as well.

A hymn of the Resurrection proclaims: "Let us embrace one another. Let those who hate us speak to us: 'Brethren, for the sake of the resurrection we will all forgive one another'· and so let us cry out: Christ rose from the dead after destroying death by death: he gives life to all . . . ."

So it is an act of love when people forgive one another. It is an act of love when they pray for each other. It is an act of love when they humble themselves before each other. In an age of anxiety and of the degradation of human nature, Christianity's gospel of God's *philanthropia* must find an analogous response in our love for one another. Indeed we "owe no one anything, except to love one another" (Rom. 13:8), as "God so loved the world that he gave his only Son, that whoever believes in him should not perish but have eternal life" (Jn. 3:16).

The Orthodox Church prays for hope, charity, and love. As a church that has suffered the brutalities of man, she pleads for sanity and understanding among the powerful of the earth, lest they recklessly destroy man, the image and the masterpiece of God. Orthodoxy's message to the Christian world can be summed up in the words of Saint Peter: "Having purified your souls by your obedience to the truth . . . love one another earnestly from the heart . . . .through the living and abiding word of God" (1 Pet. 1:22–23).

5

The Greek Orthodox in America

Because the present volume is intended primarily for readers living in the Americas, it would seem appropriate to include here a short chapter on the Greek Orthodox in America.

The Beginnings (1768–1891)

A substantial colony of some five hundred Greek Orthodox emigrated to the New World in 1768. The Greek immigrants arrived under the aegis of a Scottish physician named Andrew Turnbull and his Greek wife, Maria. The Greek colony was named New Smyrna and was located in the northeast part of the present state of Florida.

Dr. Turnbull had made plans for both a Greek Orthodox Church and a regular priest to serve the spiritual needs of his settlers. On March 31, 1767, he had petitioned the Board of Trade of England for an annual allowance of £100 for the first Greek Orthodox priest. But, as far as modern scholarship can tell, Dr. Turnbull's plans did not materialize. There is no evidence either that a Greek Orthodox priest accompanied the 1768 Greek immigrants or that a Greek Orthodox Church was established in eighteenth-century America.

In addition to the New Smyrna colonists, many Greek Orthodox merchants, traders, and refugees from Turkish persecution settled in the United States during its revolutionary and early national period. They were dispersed everywhere, from Boston to New York, as far south as New Orleans and as far west as San Francisco. In cities such as San Francisco, they attended services in Russian Orthodox churches.

The earliest Greek Orthodox church in the United States was established in 1862 in the seaport city of Galveston, Texas, and it was named after Saints Constantine and Helen. Even though the church was founded by Greeks, it served the spiritual needs of other Orthodox Christians, such as Russians, Serbians, and Syrians. It passed into the hands of the Serbians, who split with the Greeks. The Greeks then established their own church several decades later; but knowledge of the early years of the Galveston Greek Orthodox community is very limited. Neither the number of Greek Orthodox parishioners there nor the name of the first priest is known. The first known Greek Orthodox priest of this community was an Athenian named Theokletos Triantafylides, who had received his theological training in the Moscow Ecclesiastical Academy and had taught in Russia before joining the North American Russian Orthodox Mission. Versed in both Greek and Slavonic, he was able to minister successfully to all Orthodox Christians.

Knowledge of the second Greek community in the United States is more extensive. It was organized in 1864 in the port city of New Orleans. Like the Galveston community, the second one was also founded by merchants. For three years (1864–1867) services were held irregularly and in different buildings. Then in 1867 the congregation moved to its own church structure, named after the Holy Trinity. It was erected through the generosity of the philanthropist Marinos Benakis, who donated the lot and $500, and of Demetrios N. and John N. Botasis, cotton merchants who together contributed $1,000.

The church was located at 1222 Dorgenois Street and for several years it became the object of generosity not only of Greeks but of Syrians, Russians, and other Slavs. In addition to Greeks, the board of trustees included one Syrian and one Slav. Notwithstanding the predominance of Greeks on the board, the minutes were written in English and for a while it served as a pan-Orthodox Church.

The early Holy Trinity Church was a simple wooden rectangular edifice 60 feet long and 35 feet wide. The major icons of the iconostasis were painted by Constantine Lesbios, who completed his work in February of 1872. The name of the first parish priest is unknown, but it is believed that a certain uncanonical clergyman named Agapios Honcharenko, of the Russian Orthodox mission in America, served the community for three years (1864–1867). In 1867 the congregation moved to its permanent church and appointed its first regular priest, Stephen Andreades, who had been invited from Greece. He had a successful ministry from 1867 to 1875, when the archimandrite Gregory Yiayias arrived to replace him.

The New Orleans congregation also acquired its own parish house; a small library, which included books in Greek, Latin, and Slavonic; and a cemetery.

The number of churches in the second half of the nineteenth century corresponded to the number of Greek Orthodox communities, which were concentrated in cities. Up to 1891 there were approximately twenty-five hundred Greek Orthodox in the United States; from then on, there was a substantial increase in immigration. In 1891 and later many Greek Orthodox churches were founded in large cities such as New York, Chicago, San Francisco, and Boston, and in many smaller cities and towns such as Washington, D.C.; Newark, New Jersey; Ipswich, Massachusetts; Omaha, Nebraska; Pensacola, Florida; and Moline, Illinois. In the course of thirty-one years (1891–1922), 139 new Greek Orthodox congregations were organized in the United States and two in Canada.

The following ten churches were the earliest in the United States after the two in Galveston and New Orleans.

> Holy Trinity, New York City (established in 1891)
> Holy Trinity, Chicago (1892)
> Annunciation (Evangelismos) of the Theotokos,
>   New York City (1893)
> Holy Trinity, Lowell, Massachusetts (1894)
> Annunciation of the Theotokos, Philadelphia (1901)
> Saint Nicholas, Newark, New Jersey (1901)
> Holy Trinity, Birmingham, Alabama (1902)
> Holy Trinity, San Francisco (1903)
> Annunciation of the Theotokos, Boston (1903)
> Saint Nicholas, St. Louis, Missouri (1904)

Why were the earliest churches named in honor of the Holy Trinity, the Annunciation, Saint Nicholas? Obviously they manifest belief in the doctrine of the Holy Trinity and the Annunciation of God's good news—the *evangelismos* of the incarnation of Christ and His appearance among men. But the Annunciation is also a popular holiday among the Greeks because it is linked with Greek Independence Day. The use of Saint Nicholas' name indicates that a humble and philanthropic, not necessarily an intellectual, Church Father is held in high esteem by the faithful.

Of the 141 churches founded in the United States between 1862 and 1922,

30 were named after the Annunciation of the Theotokos
24 after the Holy Trinity
19 after the Dormition *(koimesis)* of the Theotokos
15 after Saint George
13 after Saints Constantine and Helen
9 after Saint Nicholas
7 after Saint Demetrios
6 after Saint John the Baptist
4 after God's Wisdom (Hagia Sophia)
4 after Saint Spyridon
2 after All Saints and
2 after the Holy Apostles

The rest were named in honor of various other individual saints. While the number of Greek Orthodox communities was substantial, the faithful in the New World were like a flock without a shepherd. For three decades the Church was beset by numerous problems and a great deal of instability. Why?

A Flock Without a Shepherd (1891–1918)

By 1913 the Greek Orthodox population of the United States had increased to nearly a quarter of a million; and by 1922 it was estimated at between 300,000 and half a million. For example, the Massachusetts Bureau of Immigration put the number at 350,000 and the census of 1920 reported 175,972 foreign-born Greeks in the United States. However, considering the new arrivals between 1920 and 1922 as well as those

Greek Orthodox born in America between 1862 and 1922, it seems probable that by 1922, when the Church was organized into an archdiocese, the Greek Orthodox in the United States numbered indeed approximately half a million.

Up to the year 1908, the Greek Orthodox communities of the American diaspora were under the spiritual aegis of the Ecumenical Patriarchate of Constantinople. But owing to the uncertainties in Turkey and the wave of Turkish nationalism under the Young Turks, as well as to international political events, Patriarch Ioakim III, in agreement with the holy synod of the Patriarchate, issued a tome (letter) on March 8, 1908, which placed the Greek Orthodox churches in America under the jurisdiction of the autocephalous Church of Greece. Nevertheless, the churches in America remained fairly independent, and no effective supervision existed for several years.

The Church in America—it can be referred to as one Church because of the unity of faith, worship, and ethics—was in flux for several reasons. Most of the Greek Orthodox were immigrants whose ultimate goal was not to make their home permanently in the New World, but to accumulate enough savings to be able to return to the motherland. Thus they were not interested in supporting churches in America.

For these and for cultural, linguistic, and national reasons, the Greek Orthodox in America during the first quarter of the twentieth century strongly resisted assimilation. But it was more than ethnic pride that made them resist Americanization. They found the United States not simply a "melting pot," whatever that expression may mean, but a "pressure cooker." In the first quarter of this century, there was in the United States a wave of antagonism to foreigners, which did little to encourage adjustment or assimilation. There was an evident dichotomy between what the Constitution proclaimed and what actually took place. According to many accounts, the country was interested only in the labor and sweat of its newcomers, not in their presence in its established society. Many immigrants resented the paternalism of some religious organizations, immigration authorities, and social or sectarian societies of various kinds, which directly or indirectly were forcing them to adopt American ways. One of the writers of the period summarized the Greek reaction as follows:

A great deal is being said and written regarding the Americanization or assimilation of the immigrants that seems strange. Some of the heated utterances sound like the nationalistic theories of the Pan-Germans or the Pan-Slavists. If the various races are to be forced to forget all their racial peculiarities and characteristics, customs, usages, and language, and to adopt American ways instead, the result will be disappointing. Whenever a people is forced to accept, willingly or unwillingly, a certain course of action, the result has usually been the opposite of what was desired . . . . Even the word "Americanization" sounds strange to many ears; it sounds like suppression, force.

The American religious mind of the late nineteenth and early twentieth centuries was determined "to maintain the United States as a homogeneous, evangelical enterprise." The new immigrants were viewed as a threat to the established society. Thus there was a great deal of effort to Americanize them through the values and creeds of the various established religious groups. A modern author rightly emphasizes that

The immigrant to America . . . was to be simply raw material for Americanization—a faceless mass of mankind unable to make any contribution to America beyond sweat. Americanization was paternalistic and aimed at imparting to the newly arrived the tried and true gospel of the American Civil Religion.

But the treatment of the immigrant by the "natives" was anything but Christian. Leroy Hodges, a commissioner of immigration, in 1912 described the "evangelical" way as follows:

Churches supported by American Protestants located in the immigrant colonies refuse to receive the recent immigrants in their buildings as the native Americans are received, and some of them resort to the practice of holding services for them in barns, stores, and other such places, posing the while before the public as ardent "settlement workers." Some ministers have gone so far as to make the statement that the recent immigrants are a "lot of filthy cattle," with which they

> do not care to litter up their churches . . . . Not only are they
> not assisting in the Americanization of the new citizens, but
> they are engendering an opposition against the institutions
> upon which the future of the United States rests.

Nevertheless, despite the immigrant's reluctance to accept
Americanization, with the passing of time, the establishment
of a family, the exposure to new ideas, new institutions, and
a new environment, and familiarity with the language, much
assimilation was achieved. Besides the threat of being prose-
lytized, the problems the Greek Orthodox encountered during
the period under discussion were many and diverse. They had
to overcome a great deal of prejudice; and they had to work
hard and long in order to improve socially and financially. Since
most of them came from the rural stratum of Greek society,
from remote villages and small towns, many suffered from an
inferiority complex. Others, through ignorance of the language
and the laws of the country, found themselves in the courts.

A happy exception in the contest among some denominations
to convert the Greeks was the Episcopal Church. For centuries
there has been an affinity between the Orthodox Church and
the Anglican Communion, and the Episcopal Church provided
much help to the early Orthodox when they were in need of
buildings for Church services. It was the official policy of the
Episcopal Church not to conduct missionary activity among the
Orthodox.

In retrospect, one may suspect that many American Christians viewed the Greek Orthodox as pagans. Some years ago,
I was asked to lecture to a congregation in an "enlightened"
New England town. Before I was introduced by the pastor, I
was approached by a group of ladies and asked various questions. A delightful middle-aged lady asked me: "Do you still
believe in Zeus?" If some "natives" could raise such a question
in 1967, one can imagine the kind of ignorance about Orthodox
Christianity that prevailed in the early twentieth century.

Many Greek Orthodox, because of an inferiority complex,
for business purposes, or in order to avoid discrimination,
changed their names (though many Greek names had already
been shortened or changed arbitrarily by immigration officers).

Thus a Papadopoulos became Brown, a Konstantinides was shortened to Constant, Anagnostopoulos emerged as Agnew, Papanikolaou as Papps, and so on. There are many of Greek origin who have adopted names such as Williams, Johnson, Adams, Peterson, Bell, Kress, Nickolson, Johns, Carr, Larry, Lorant, Papps, Pepps, Moore, Stance, Pelican, Ross, and Meyers, Allen, Anagnost, Anton, Apostle, and Apostol.

Notwithstanding the proselytizing by several Protestant denominations and other religious groups, as a whole the Greek Orthodox remained faithful to their ancestral faith and their Greek heritage. In order to preserve their culture and traditions they established fraternities, social clubs, Greek language schools, newspapers (two dailies), and magazines.

Many Greeks joined a fraternity before they joined a church—some because they preferred the social life to the religious, others because a fraternity was easy to form and to sustain, while the organization of a church required not only a priest and a church building but regular financial support. Several fraternities played an important role in the organization of the Church. The third paragraph of Article One of a certain fraternity's statement of its objectives declares that one of its purposes was "to preserve the Greek Orthodox Church and to develop and propagate educational and moral doctrines among the Greek compatriots residing in the United States and Canada."

One of the Church's major problems was that she was without any bishops to coordinate the various communities and to direct the destiny of the Church. There was much individualism, dissension, and lack of orientation. The 141 communities were like 141 ancient Greek city-states in an American archipelago. Some churches were social clubs rather than religious communities. To be sure, each congregation usually had its own priest, but priests were expected to administer the sacraments and conduct funerals rather than to lead the congregation, which usually was under the control of a lay board of trustees. The priest, often ill-educated, had come to America for the same purpose as his parishioners, and he was frequently at the mercy of the community, especially the board of trustees, which had appointed him. It has been rightly observed that in Greek parishes until 1922 "congregationalism reigned supreme in an episcopal church."

While undoubtedly many were concerned with the Church as the provider of spiritual and religious values, others were only traditionally Orthodox, attending the Liturgy on Christmas or Easter Sunday, or religious services conducted for some of their friends—a baptism, wedding, funeral, or memorial service. Church attendance was very poor. Nevertheless, it was due to the zeal of certain dedicated laymen that most of the churches were established. For example, Holy Trinity Cathedral of New York, established in 1891, was the work of lay members of the Athena Society. They applied to the holy synod of Greece, which appointed Paisios Ferentinos the first priest of the New York cathedral. Services were held for several years in a hall or in a rented church building until 1904, when the congregation was able to build its own structure at 153 East 72nd Street.

The way the New York cathedral was organized was more or less standard, and it served as the prototype for the establishment of later churches. First, a group of dedicated laymen would get together to determine whether there were enough Greek Orthodox to support a church. As soon as they secured the support of some fifty families, they would apply to the state for a charter of incorporation under titles such as Hellenic Eastern Orthodox Church of ———— or Greek Orthodox Church of ————. The second step was to apply to the Ecumenical Patriarchate or to the Church of Greece, and sometimes to the Patriarchate of Alexandria, for a priest. The choice of the church to which the application for a priest was sent was often determined either by the political affiliation of the applicants or the place of their origin. Greeks from the mainland usually applied to the holy synod of Greece, while Greeks from Asia Minor, Thrace, and other regions usually directed their application to Constantinople.

As soon as a priest was available, the committee would seek to rent a hall or a church building, usually from the Episcopal Church. As a rule the congregation would move to its own building within a few years. Though the Church welcomed all Greek Orthodox, not all were supporting members. As already stated, the concern of many was to save enough to return to the motherland. Thus, though there were many Greek Orthodox, there were few churches and contributing members. This explains why the clergy were poorly paid and the churches in great debt and uncertain about their future.

A turning point in the history of the Church occurred in August of 1918, when the archbishop of Athens, Meletios Metaxakis, arrived in New York to study the problems of the Greek Orthodox in America. He was accompanied by Bishop Alexandros, the titular bishop of Rodostolou (who later became Archbishop Alexander of America), by Archimandrite Chrysostom Papadopoulos (a renowned ecclesiastical historian who later became archbishop of Athens), and by a few laymen. Meletios Metaxakis was determined to bring order out of the chaotic conditions that prevailed in the Church. In the past, several requests had been sent to the mother churches for a bishop and for more concern for the church of the diaspora, but with no definite results. For example, the Greek consul general in New York City, Demetrios N. Botasis, in a report to the Greek government dated July 15, 1904, made a strong case to the Greek Ministry of Foreign Affairs requesting its intervention with the synod of the Church of Greece for the appointment of a bishop. But no bishop was sent.

The lack of initiative on the part of both the Church of Constantinople and the Church of Greece reveals what happens when a church is not a free institution or when it is tied to the state. Both churches were subject to the internal problems of their respective states, and both were prevented from acting by nonreligious considerations. The Church of Greece was divided between the loyalists and liberals, especially in the period of 1914 to 1918, and the good bishops had no time to devote to the problems of the immigrants. The Ecumenical Patriarchate was continuously under the threat of the sword of the Turks. When the Young Turks came to power in 1908, they were determined to expel all Christian minorities, including the historic Ecumenical Patriarchate. It was primarily because of the uncertainties caused by neo-Turkish nationalism that the Patriarchate could not concern itself with the problems of the American Church and issued, in March of 1908, the tome that placed the Greek Orthodox in America under the jurisdiction of the autocephalous Church of Greece.

However one of the reasons why both the Ecumenical Patriarchate and the Church of Greece were reluctant to appoint a bishop for the Greek Orthodox faithful in America may have been canonical. Canon law forbids the appointment of a bishop in a province or district where a canonical bishop already exists, and there were in the New World Orthodox bishops of the Moscow Patriarchate. It was not the first time that Greeks had been under the spiritual guidance of Russian Orthodox. To be sure, some or even many Greeks may not have been happy under the Moscow Patriarchate. But it is rather unjust to blame "Greek nationalism" for the reluctance of the Greek faithful to accept Russian leadership. It may have been inefficiency, lack of unity, and turmoil within the Russian church that persuaded the Greeks to seek their own leadership.

Whatever the reasons, the first Greek Orthodox bishop arrived in the United States in 1918, and it was in that year that the hierarchy of the church began to organize the Greek Orthodox communities in the States.

Bringing the Flock Together (1918–1930)

It was amid chaotic conditions that the first bishop was appointed to proclaim concord and love and to consolidate the Greek Orthodox communities into a united Greek Orthodox archdiocese. Even though Archbishop Meletios stayed in the United States only three months, he had a permanent impact. His work was primarily that of fostering contacts among the clergy, the community leaders, and the faithful. He was a magnetic figure, and he drew to himself opposing factions.

The most important accomplishment of Archbishop Meletios was the creation of the Synodic Trusteeship (Synodike Epitropeia) and the appointment of Bishop Alexander as his own and the synod's personal representative. Thus, since 1918, the Church has been under episcopal leadership. But from 1918 to 1922, several cataclysmic events in the motherland greatly affected the history of the Church in the New World. During this time, Greece was racked by a struggle between the supporters of the crown and those of the political leader Venizelos.

The episcopal representative in the United States was tied to the destiny of his superior in Greece. So when Meletios Metaxakis was deposed as archbishop of Athens because of political developments in Greece, his representative in America found himself in a very difficult situation. Upon his deposition from office as archbishop of Athens, Meletios sought refuge among the Greek Orthodox in America. While Meletios was on his way to New York City, Bishop Alexander was asked to return to Greece. But, with the support of Meletios, Alexander refused to obey the new archbishop in Greece, placed himself under the jurisdiction of the Ecumenical Patriarchate, and decided to stay and carry on his religious duties.

While in America, Meletios acted as the canonical archbishop of Athens, and Alexander served as his auxiliary. For almost a year they cooperated closely in the organization of the Church, in the pacification and the union of split communities, and in the advancement of the Greek Orthodox in America.

Meletios was a visionary and a dynamic person. In the short time that he stayed in the United States he accomplished a great deal. On August 11, 1921, he invited the lay and clerical leaders of the communities to the first congress of clergy and laity, which was held from September 13 to 15, 1921, in the Holy Trinity Cathedral of New York. One of the major decisions of this congress was to seek the incorporation of all Greek Orthodox communities into The Greek Orthodox Archdiocese of North and South America. A constitution was drawn up and the charter of the archdiocese was issued by the state of New York on September 19, 1921.

In addition, Meletios aspired to have a clergy educated in the United States not only in theology but also in the English language, able to guide old and young alike, to lead and to preserve the church in multisectarian America. Thus he established Saint Athanasios Greek Orthodox Seminary in Astoria, New York. Furthermore, he organized a "philanthropic treasury" for the poor; he edited a weekly journal, the *Ecclesiastical Herald,* and promoted ecumenical relations between the Orthodox and non-Orthodox Churches, the Episcopal Church in particular. The Greek Orthodox continued to be especially friendly with the Episcopal Church. As early as 1919 Archbishop Alexander attended an Episcopal ordination in Lancaster, Pennsylvania, as an observer. An Episcopal priest and influential author reported that "after the separation of a thousand years, practical union has come; therefore we have a special duty of friendliness to the members of our sister churches of the East. We can cooperate with them in reaching their own people and help them to be faithful to their great church."

The same writer records that Archbishop Alexander had expressed "his willingness to enter into an agreement by which our clergy may be licensed to minister to his people where their priests are far away."

Because of his excellent reputation and his activity among non-Orthodox Church organizations and agencies, Archbishop Meletios was awarded several honors by American institutions, including universities.

One of Meletios' efforts was to mediate on behalf of the Christian minorities in Turkey, which since 1908 had been undergoing relentless persecutions. The genocide inflicted upon the Armenians by the Turks had moved many Americans, but little had been done to save the Christian minorities in Anatolia. Charles Evans Hughes was a champion of the Christian minorities there as long as he was outside the government. But when as secretary of state he was pressed for action against Turkey, Hughes forgot his idealistic principles and became a "political realist." In a letter dated December 8, 1921, Meletios pleaded with him to protect the minorities in Turkey.

Despite the fact that many Greek Orthodox had numerous personal and family financial obligations, they responded generously to several humanitarian causes. Of course, for many, one of the obligations was to provide dowries or financial assistance for their sisters back home. It was not unusual for brothers to remain single or to postpone their marriage in order to accumulate enough money for their sisters. Parents and brothers in the motherland also received liberal contributions from their sons and relatives in America.

The Greek Orthodox responded generously to several drives in behalf of war refugees, victims of earthquakes, and various philanthropic causes. Among the needy, the Greek Orthodox included brethren of the Russian Church who had fled their motherland during and following the 1917 revolution. Bishop Alexander issued a special encyclical stressing the need for assistance to all, including people outside his jurisdiction.

Another turning point in the history of the Church in America was the election of Archbishop Meletios Metaxakis to the throne of the Ecumenical Patriarchate of Constantinople, on November 25, 1921, as Meletios IV. In his farewell encyclical to the Greek Americans, dated December 31, 1921, Meletios appealed for mutual forgiveness and concord among the Greek Orthodox and enjoined them to unite around the person of Bishop Alexander. He arrived in Constantinople on January 24, 1922.

Meletios was an impatient and sometimes careless man. Of course, he had realized that in the Church of America the Ecumenical Patriarchate possessed a substantial power, both moral and economic. Thus one of Meletios' major decisions as patriarch was to annul the 1908 tome and thus bring the Church of America under the jurisdiction of the Ecumenical Patriarchate. This was confirmed by the Patriarchate's synod and was conveyed to the Church in America on March 1, 1922. Conditions had not changed either in Greece or in Turkey. The argument that the Church in America was again placed under the Patriarchate because conditions in Greece were ominous is not convincing. The transfer was the arbitrary act of a dynamic person who knew how to turn events to his advantage.

Two months later, on May 11, 1922, Patriarch Meletios announced to Bishop Alexander that the holy synod and he had elected Alexander archbishop and had elevated the Church in America to an archdiocese. The archdiocese was to include three diocesan districts, with their sees in Boston, Chicago, and San Francisco.

Archbishop Alexander had been in the United States for four years and had firsthand knowledge of the problems as well as the potentialities of his flock. But from the very beginning he had encountered several major problems. When he had refused to acknowledge the new archbishop of Athens and his synod (which had deposed Archbishop Meletios Metaxakis) and to return to Greece as he had been ordered, the synod of

Greece had appointed the metropolitan of Sparta and Monem-vasia, Germanos Trojanos, as its exarch in North and South America; he arrived in New York in June 1921, while Arch-bishop Meletios was still in the country. Thus there were two archbishops: Alexander, who owed his authority to the Ecu-menical Patriarchate of Constantinople, and Germanos, who had been appointed as exarch by the Church of Greece.

Priests and communities were now divided not only between Royalist and Venizelist churches but also between churches that belonged to two ecclesiastical jurisdictions. Even though in the beginning the breach seemed to widen, the majority of the congregations finally rallied to Archbishop Alexander, who gained more and more communities after the organization of the Church as an archdiocese. In the meantime the relations between the Ecumenical Patriarchate and the Church of Greece improved, and Metropolitan Germanos Trojanos was recalled to Greece in January of 1923. This helped tremendously to heal the schism between the communities, most of which came under Alexander's jurisdiction, while a few remained independent.

Another difficulty for Archbishop Alexander was to bring the scattered communities, which had been accustomed to self-government and complete independence from any authority except that of the membership, under the aegis and authority of a centralized archdiocese. Closely related was the arch-bishop's right to appoint priests to the congregations. But this right collided with a practice of long standing, according to which the board of trustees of a congregation sought out and appointed its priest. It was very difficult for the laity to un-derstand the theological teaching concerning the nature of the Church, the episcopal office, and its function. After decades without a bishop and in isolation from the mainstream of Or-thodoxy, the Greek Orthodox in America had grown into in-dependent congregations. It took more than twenty years of hard work to bring the communities into the fold of the archdiocese.

In June 1923, a few months after the departure of Germanos Trojanos, the Ecumenical Patriarchate elected two bishops for the Church in North America. Philaretos Ioannides was appointed bishop of Chicago for the Middle West and Ioakim Alexopoulos was ordained bishop of Boston for the New England states. They were not meant to be auxiliary bishops under Archbishop Alexander. All three were to constitute a small synod, which was augmented four years later when, in 1927, Kallistos Papageorgakopoulos was ordained and appointed bishop of San Francisco for the Western states.

Notwithstanding the new arrangement, with one archbishop and three bishops, the decade of the 1920s continued to be turbulent. The election of the three bishops did not satisfy the congregations that had sided with the Royalist party. In fact, all bishops were considered Venizelists. The division assumed large proportions when a Royalist metropolitan named Vasilios Kombopoulos arrived in the United States to head the Royalist communities. Metropolitan Vasilios acted unilaterally and established the Autocephalous Greek Orthodox Church of the United States and Canada.

The question has been raised again and again: What kind of man was Alexander? Was he the proper hierarch to lead widely dispersed and highly individualistic congregations in America? These questions cannot be answered in a brief essay, but a few observations may be made. To be sure, he has been criticized severely, but he has been held responsible for things that were beyond his control, and a close study of his encyclicals and private correspondence reveals that Alexander was devoted to the Church as well as to the Ecumenical Patriarchate. Even though much of his time was devoted to administrative duties, to exerting every effort to unite congregations and bring dissident communities under the aegis of the archdiocese, Archbishop Alexander was greatly concerned with humanitarian and philanthropic programs. Broad-minded and tolerant, he was a good man. It has been rightly observed that "Alexander fought courageously. If he lost heart and erred at the end of this painful decade, it was because every struggle has an end and a victim."

Alexander had some failures. Despite many efforts to maintain Saint Athanasios Seminary, it had to close its doors two years after its opening for lack of financial support. It was not that the Greek communities could not support a seminary;

rather it was the dissensions in the American Church that affected the financial condition of the school. He failed also to unite all the communities and to assert the authority of the archdiocese. But who could have succeeded under the circumstances? Following more than thirty years of ecclesiastical anarchy, how was it possible for one or even four bishops to gather the widely scattered flock into one fold? Nevertheless, Alexander laid the foundations, and the unity of the Church he sought was achieved much more easily under his successor.

During Archbishop Alexander's primacy the second and third Clergy-Laity Congresses were held. The second was held in New York in August 1922, and the third in Chicago in October 1927. Those assemblies served not only to enhance the authority of the archdiocese but also as links between congregations and their members.

The first quarter of the twentieth century was full of dramatic happenings for the Greek nation and its Church. In particular, the third decade was a decade of cataclysmic episodes that permanently affected the life of millions of Greek Orthodox. After more than 3,000 years in Asia Minor, the Greeks were permanently uprooted from there. Chauvinistic Turkey became determined to expel from her territories all Christian minorities, whether Armenians, Greeks, or others. Thus hundreds of thousands were expelled from their homes, while many more were put to the sword.

More than once, Archbishop Alexander rallied his flock in America to help refugees, orphans, and the many destitute who fled the Turkish madness. From 1919 to 1930, the last year of his stay in the United States, Alexander wrote numerous encyclicals and promoted many philanthropic causes. These documents reveal that the archbishop appealed for material contributions to the Christian minorities expelled from Pontos and other regions of Asia Minor. He wrote encyclicals and personal letters to help orphans and orphanages; poor students, needy professors, and destitute priests; the Ecumenical Patriarchate; the Near East Relief Fund; victims of earthquakes in Greece; sanatoria; the American Red Cross; and unemployed and poor miners in the United States. He also had a deep concern for the poor, for schools, and for educational programs.

Of course, there is no way of knowing how effective all those appeals were, and there is no concrete evidence of how much actual material assistance was given to the needy. What is known, however, is that these documents reflect a man full of empathy and active concern.

Archbishop Alexander also established in the archdiocese the Office of Relief of the Greek Archdiocese of North and South America, with a board of twelve and himself as chairman. The purposes of the office of relief, located at 215 West 23rd Street in New York, were to provide assistance to all those entering or leaving the country; to provide financial as well as other support to immigrants who for some reason were held in custody or in prison; to find housing for those newcomers who desired to stay in New York until ready to move on to their destination; to counsel immigrants concerning the laws of the country and to assist those in conflict with the law; to organize classes and meetings for the orientation of the newly arrived; to visit hospitals and give help to the sick. How effective this office was and to what degree it carried out its functions is very difficult to say.

In 1929, there were close to 200 Greek Orthodox congregations in the United States. Of these, 133 were under the jurisdiction of Archbishop Alexander; 50 were under the so-called Autocephalous Greek Orthodox Church of the United States and Canada, headed by the deposed Archbishop Vasilios Kombopoulos; a few were totally independent; and a few more, which followed the Julian, or Old Style, Calendar, were under either the Patriarchate of Jerusalem or that of Alexandria. Of course, the main problem was to unite the two major bodies. And this became the common concern of the Churches of Constantinople and Athens.

Patriarch Photios II of Constantinople, in agreement with Archbishop Chrysostom Papadopoulos of Athens and with the cooperation of the Greek government, decided to recall all bishops from America, including Archbishop Vasilios Kombopoulos, who was to be restored to his canonical status. In order to facilitate the transition and prevent new schisms, the Partiarchate appointed Damaskenos, the capable metropolitan of Corinth, as exarch of the Ecumenical Patriarchate and as interim head of the canonical Greek archdiocese. He proved a shrewd arbitrator.

Damaskenos arrived in the United States on May 20, 1930, and after he had visited the President of the United States and other civil authorities, he issued an irenic encyclical to all Greek Orthodox congregations, explaining the reason for his arrival. He met with Archbishop Alexander and the other bishops, to whom Damaskenos conveyed the Patriarchate's decision.

Alexander at first appeared conciliatory but soon hardened his position. In fact, on May 26, 1930, he issued his own encyclical, expressing his feelings of disappointment over Damaskenos' tactics. He stressed that the exarch's activities were unwarranted and appealed to his flock for intervention by writing to Patriarch Photios, the Greek government, and to Damaskenos on his behalf.

Nonetheless Damaskenos, who proceeded methodically and rather cautiously in the very beginning, was determined to carry out his mandate. When Alexander refused to resign, Damaskenos cabled the Patriarch and the synod asking for more drastic measures against Alexander. The result was that Alexander was officially deposed by the Patriarch.

Furthermore the Patriarchate accepted Damaskenos' second recomendation, which called for the election of Athenagoras Spyrou, metropolitan of Kerkyra (Corfu), as the new archbishop of the American archdiocese. In addition, Damaskenos proposed a new constitution, which favored a more centralized archdiocese, the abolition of the synodic system, and the appointment of auxiliary bishops rather than autonomous heads of diocesan districts.

Damaskenos' final report reveals that the Church in America was evolving along independent lines, that there was a great deal of assimilation, and that there was a great need for educated clergymen who would inspire not only religious enthusiasm but a sense of ethnic pride and of loyalty to the Ecumenical Patriarchate. He had an excellent awareness of the tendencies in Greek Orthodoxy, and his lengthy report reflects the issues, trends, dangers, and orientation of the Greek Orthodox in the New World. While Alexander favored more autonomy and was cognizant of the American realities, Damaskenos emphasized the need for patriarchal control and stronger ties between the Greek Orthodox in America and the motherland.

Deposed, left with few friends, and disillusioned, Alexander yielded to the decision of the Patriarchate and agreed to leave the United States. He was appointed metropolitan of Kerkyra, whose metropolitan in the meantime had been elected to succeed him in America.

This change took place at a time when conditions were greatly improving in the Greek communities in America. Indeed, it illustrates what has been observed by historians: That not only major revolutions but social changes of a less drastic nature occur when things start to improve, and not under the most depressed conditions. Archbishop Alexander rightly complained that Damaskenos had arrived when things were becoming better.

Whatever the future evaluation may be of the archbishop, the fact is that Alexander "fought the good fight" and accomplished a great deal under ominous circumstances. The Greek Orthodox should cherish his memory in grateful acknowledgement of a very dedicated ministry.

In the early years of its establishment, the Church gave the immigrants moral support, cultural reinforcement, and a sense of belonging together, of dignity and self-esteem. Through its priests and services, the Church stood by the immigrant in the hours of birth and death, gave comfort in sickness and encouragement in moments of anxiety and catastrophe.

Order in the House (1931–1948)

The departure of Archbishop Alexander from America and the arrival of his successor brought to an end the most anomalous period in the Church's history in America and introduced a new era. It seems, however, that while the person and the ministry of Alexander have been underrated, the success of Athenagoras has been overstressed. Admittedly, the handsome appearance and Olympian personality of Archbishop Athenagoras magnetized the people and left behind a legend.

Elected on August 13, 1930, the new archbishop arrived in New York City on February 24, 1931. As already stated, the climate in the Church had improved considerably. Dissident churches still existed, but on the whole the congregations were eager to forget the conflicts of the past and their political commitments, and to cooperate for the progress of all.

Athenagoras was a diplomat, often a politician, and an excellent public relations man. One of his first undertakings upon arrival was to visit President Herbert Hoover, other political, religious, and civic dignitaries, and of course, his own flock. Early in his ministry he visited some fifty congregations. His strength derived from the way he approached and captivated people. He had little sympathy for abstract theology and theoretical arguments. His encyclicals reveal him a pragmatist. He imposed his authority and won over even his adversaries by a fatherly manner rather than by any profound thought or arguments.

One of the major changes introduced in the Church was a new constitution. The synodic system that had governed the Church from 1922 to 1930 was abolished, and the bishops were no longer autonomous heads of dioceses but titulars, serving as auxiliaries to the archbishop. During Athenagoras' primacy there were five diocesan districts, each with one auxiliary bishop, in New York, Boston, Chicago, San Francisco, and Charlotte, North Carolina. By 1931, there were 220 priests with an equal number of parishes and a Greek Orthodox population of some 750,000 persons. In 1934, there were 250 priests, more priests than congregations.

During the Great Depression several small Greek Orthodox churches were closed down because many of their parishioners had moved to larger cities seeking employment. Other churches were threatened with foreclosures or bankruptcies because of large mortgages. On several occasions the archdiocese moved to prevent such failures. For example, the communities of Clinton and Lawrence in Massachusetts were threatened with extinction in 1936; but local clergy-laity congresses, such as the fourth local congress of New England, held in Brockton, Massachusetts, as well as appeals from Archbishop Athenagoras, provided the necessary money for the security of these two communities, which have survived to the present day.

There is evidence that the Church as an organized body made some efforts to relieve the poor and help the needy during the Great Depression, but there is no statistical evidence concerning the type of work that was initiated by the archdiocese. The best indication of Athenagoras' concern for the destitute and the needy is a moving encyclical issued on October 20, 1932, in the name of the Central Council of the Ladies' Philoptochos Society. This encyclical, signed by the Archbishop as president of the society, ten members of the board, and two secretaries, was an excellent example of the Church's concern for human beings. It summarized the theological teachings about philanthropy and gave direction to the various chapters of the Society and to the congregations on a number of important matters, for example, where and how to seek out and help the unemployed, the sick, the orphans, the widows, the homeless, those in prison, the aged, the young immigrants who had no one to turn to for guidance, those in conflict with the law because of ignorance, and others in need.

Of course, every archbishop has issued many similar appeals, and it is difficult to say whether these appeals had any result. It was up to the individual priest and individual chapters of the Philoptochos Society to respond to the needs of their people, and the Church must have responded according to her means and ability to the needs of her people during the Great Depression.

Nevertheless, the archdiocese was criticized for not doing enough to help the poor and the unemployed. One Greek critic of the clergy wrote:

What have the clergy done for the various victims of the depression? All other churches and various social organizations have established centers for the care and relief of the poor; only our glorious orthodoxy sleeps under the mandrake and satisfies itself with a few appeals and pompous pretensions. And, what shall we say when, as we are told, clergymen are engaging in profitable enterprises, neglecting their high calling to become real estate and stock market manipulators?

In his eighteen years of ministry in America, Archbishop Athenagoras left behind several landmarks that continue to determine the destiny of the Church in America. The problems of dissent, congregational independence, and schism continued to exist for several years after his arrival. But as a result of his prodigious efforts, his enormous patience, tolerance, and persuasiveness, and his numerous contacts with and visits to the local churches, most of the dissident congregations joined the ranks of the archdiocese. Only a few communities, which followed the Julian Calendar (Old Calendarists), remained outside the archdiocese's fold.

For several years during Athenagoras's primacy, economics was one of his major problems, not only because of the Depression and the Second World War, which paralyzed many communities, but also because of the amateurish way in which the archdiocese had organized its finances. To sustain itself and maintain its programs the archdiocese had to rely on small parish contributions, collections on special occasions, and donations from a few prosperous individuals.

It was during the Eighth Clergy-Laity Congress, held in June 1942 in Philadelphia, that the grounds were laid for a stable though poor economic system. The congress adopted the *monodollarion*. Each Greek Orthodox family became obligated to contribute $1.00 a year to the archdiocese through the local parish. By modern standards the contribution was extremely low; but it provided the Church with a stable income that allowed the archdiocese to plan and partially pursue its goals. Through this system the archdiocese was able to provide salaries, very small to be sure, and support its institutions.

Athenagoras, however, is best remembered for his efforts to establish educational institutions and to provide theological training for the clergy. There were several priests with a theological degree from one of the four theological schools of Greece and the Greek Orthodox diaspora (University of Athens, University of Thessaloniki, Theological School of Chalki in Turkey, and the Holy Cross Theological School in Jerusalem). But most of the parish priests in America did not have any formal theological or even college education. Some had mastered the English language, but most had remained parochial and untouched by the new environment. There were many good immigrant priests who taught by their faith and devotion rather than by their education or special theological training.

But the membership of the Church no longer consisted only of Greek-speaking immigrants. A great number of the faithful were native born, and English was their mother tongue. The educated among them were not comfortable in a Greek-speaking church. Conditions in the Church had improved, but she continued to lose ground. Many of those who had moved upwards, both socially and educationally, left the Church. The archdiocese realized the need for educated leadership on the local level.

Holy Cross Greek Orthodox Theological Institute opened its doors in September 1937, with fourteen students and three instructors. It was placed under the deanship of the dynamic bishop of Boston, Athenagoras Kavvadas, and was located in Pomfret Center, Connecticut. It was meant to be a preparatory seminary, not a full-fledged theological school, for it possessed neither the capital nor the necessary faculty. Its graduates were to continue their theological education in one of the theological schools of Greece or of the Ecumenical Patriarchate. The Second World War, however, frustrated the original plans, and Holy Cross was reorganized as a professional five-year college and seminary. A turning point in the school's history occurred in 1946, when it moved to its present location in Brookline, Massachusetts. Undoubtedly, the establishment of Holy Cross was one of Archbishop Athenagoras's achievements, though much credit must be given to the school's first dean, who single-handedly directed its destiny for more than ten years.

The purpose of the theological institute was to give the fundamentals of theological education and much practical training for the pastoral ministry. Saint Basil's Teachers' College was established in 1944 to train teachers for Greek-language schools and for the secretarial needs of the parishes. Saint Basil's was until very recently located in Garrison, New York. It is now merged with Hellenic College, in Brookline, Massachusetts.

Admittedly, for many years both schools provided a limited education beyond high school and made no other pretensions. But both have contributed valuable services to the Orthodox Church in America. The theological school has made much progress in recent years and has received full accreditation as a graduate school of theology. Today more than three hundred Orthodox clergymen and several professional theologians are graduates of Holy Cross. Many of these have gone beyond their B.A. and B.D. training, receiving M.A.'s, Th.M.'s or other master's degrees from some of the country's finest institutions, such as Harvard, Boston University, Yale, Columbia, Fordham, Rutgers, Princeton Theological Seminary, the University of Michigan, and Duke, while several have received Th.D's or Ph.D.'s.

From 1931 to 1948, when Archbishop Athenagoras was elevated to the office of ecumenical patriarch, some one hundred new congregations were organized and several new church buildings were erected. In his ministry, the archbishop was assisted by several very dedicated bishops, one of the most industrious and totally committed being Germanos Polyzoides. He wrote many educational books in both English and Greek and hundreds of articles, and served as editor of the Church monthly, as a professor at Holy Cross, as chancellor of the archdiocese. Bishop Athenagoras Kavvadas, despite his eccentricities, was a remarkable individual. He directed the seminary and Saint Basil's and left the mark of his personality on both. A man with a mind of his own, he proved totally loyal to Archbishop Athenagoras. Bishop Kallistos, who survived the changes of 1930, remained the auxiliary bishop for the western states, which he served until his death in 1940. Less colorful but just as faithful was Bishop Eirenaios Tsourounatis, who served the midwestern states between 1943 and 1954.

Among the most important institutions organized by Archbishop Athenagoras was the Ladies' Philoptochos Society, which was set up in 1931, with central offices in the archdiocese and chapters in every congregation. Unfortunately, statistics are not available, but the Philoptochos Society has served as the right arm of the archdiocese and of each congregation in their philanthropic and social wefare responsibilities. During the Depression and Second World War years, every Philoptochos chapter contributed valuable services. The amount of work, the style, and the kind of social welfare involvement differed according to the experience and nature of each chapter. Some tended to be parochial, others cosmopolitan, in their outlook and their involvement.

The local congregation was a microcosm of both the strengths and the weaknesses of the nationwide church. Much depended on the vision, the experience, and the faith of the parish priest and the parish board of trustees. The numerous beautiful churches that came into being during the Athenagoras era were the result of local initiative—including financial initiative. Some communities were far more advanced spiritually, intellectually, socially, and financially than others.

The establishment of a theological school to train American-born students for the priesthood did not imply that the Church would soon adopt English as a liturgical tongue. The language problem existed then as it exists today. Slowly, however, but steadily, more and more English was used not only in parish life but also in the archdiocese and its institution. The Church had been bilingual from as early as the 1920s. Even then there were advocates of complete Americanization (whatever the term may mean of the Church), as there are now.

During Athenagoras's primacy, emphasis was placed on the teaching, the use, and the perpetuation of Greek not only in liturgical and sacramental life but also in many other functions of the local parish, the archdiocese, and its institutions. Athenagoras's outlook was ecumenical, but he saw no incompatibility between a Greek-speaking Church and an English-speaking environment. It was a deep appreciation of the Greek language and culture rather than chauvinism or unrealistic romanticism that made him an ardent advocate of Greek in the life of Church.

In order to preserve the language and the Greek heritage, the Church insisted on the founding of a Greek school in every community. In 1931 Archbishop Athenagoras established the Supreme Board of Education, which was expected not only to coordinate Greek education in the various parishes but also to promote the teaching of Greek in public schools. This board has been the least successful department of the archdiocese. It has engaged in much rhetoric and little initiative or concrete activity. For several years the board was also in charge of catechetical education, but the two branches of education were later divided into two separate departments. Both received a new impetus and were more effectively organized under the primacy of Athenagoras's successor.

In the course of almost two decades, Athenagoras made many friends among the non-Orthodox. He was highly respected by President Harry S. Truman. When Athenagoras was elected ecumenical patriarch in 1948 and had to move to Istanbul, President Truman provided his private plane to transport the new patriarch to his see, in acknowledgement of the importance of the office that Athenagoras was to occupy. Both the Orthodox Church in America and the Ecumenical Patriarchate became better known and more influential because of the stature and the contributions of Athenagoras.

Growth and Spiritual Awakening (1948–1960)

Before the departure of the new patriarch for Istanbul, Athenagoras Kavvadas, the bishop of Boston, was appointed *locum tenens*. While many had expected that Bishop Kavvadas would be elected the new archbishop, Patriarch Athenagoras bestowed upon him the titular dignity of metropolitan of Philadelphia and soon after appointed him to act as a liaison between the Ecumenical Patriarchate and the Church of Greece. It was not the best reward for a bishop who had been loyal and industrious for several decades. Bishop Kavvadas was not elected archbishop of the Church in America because he was suspected of independent tendencies. The patriarch, well known for his arbitrary and political maneuvers, was afraid that Kavvadas might seek the establishment of an autocephalous church in the Americas.

Bishop Athenagoras Kavvadas was succeeded as *locum tenens* by another widely experienced man, Germanos Polyzoides, titular bishop of Nyssa, who had served the Church in America since the early 1920s. While many had expected that, since Kavvadas had been passed over, Germanos Polyzoides would surely become the new head of the Church in America, it was announced that Metropolitan Timothy of Rhodes had been elected the third archbishop of the Greek archdiocese. But Timothy died while in Istanbul preparing for his new position. For the second time, Bishop Germanos of Nyssa was appointed *locum tenens* and for the second time he was by-passed. Why did the patriarch not appoint one of his former close collaborators to the office of archbishop? It seems that injustice was done to both Athenagoras Kavvadas and Germanos Polyzoides.

On October 11, 1949, Michael Konstantinides, metropolitan of Corinth, was elected archbishop of the Greek Orthodox Church of the Americas, and he arrived in New York on December 15, 1949. He was an excellent choice. Michael was a theologian with a profound mind, deep faith and commitment, and wide experience. He had served the Church in various capacities and had headed the Church in Corinth for more than ten years.

Nevertheless, the immediate reaction to Michael's election was not favorable, especially among several young archimandrites in America. Some were afraid that it would take a long time for Michael to become acquainted with the problems of the Church here. Others accused him of fundamentalism and austere manners.

Archbishop Michael proved to be a great and inspiring leader. While others laid the foundations and yet others erected the building, Michael provided the goods with which the structure was filled. In his ministry he stressed religious renaissance and emphasized the need for a rediscovery of the spiritual, or religious, dimensions of the Church as an organization and as the organism of Christ, on both the national and the local levels. He was a genuinely religious man with deep Biblical interests. From an early age he was devoted to learning and writing. He was the author of several books and the translator into modern Greek of such books as *The Imitation of Christ,* by Thomas à Kempis, and *My Life in Christ,* by John of Krostadt. He knew other Christian traditions as well as Orthodoxy. He had spent several years in Russia and twelve years in England.

A forceful and Christocentric preacher (though many complained of his lengthy encyclicals), Michael left behind the memory of an archbishop who inspired his flock with religious faith, zeal, and commitment. From the very beginning he proved innovative. Within one year he visited 107 congregations in the United States and Canada, and six months later he visited the Greek Orthodox of Latin America, who had never before been visited by an Orthodox bishop. Within months following his visit to South America, a bishop was ordained for the Orthodox there.

Through Archbishop Michael's efforts the Tenth Clergy-Laity Congress, held in November 1950 in St. Louis, adopted the *dekadollarion*, the $10 annual obligation of each Greek Orthodox family to the archdiocese. It was a salutary financial step, which contributed to the reorganization of the archdiocese. The finances of the Church have been on a firm ground ever since. Under Michael's initiative the department of religious education was totally reorganized and placed in the hands of professional religious educators. The first serious Sunday School manuals were published in the 1950s.

Another "first" of Michael's decade was the establishment of a formal national organization whose ultimate goal was to bring the young into the fold of the Church. Michael was particularly proud of the Greek Orthodox Youth of America (GOYA), and rightly so. Many of today's leaders on the archdiocesan as well as the local level were raised in the spirit of Michael's GOYA. Michael's sincerity, his idealism, and his devotion to Christian values are indelibly imprinted in the minds and hearts of the new generation of Greek Orthodox. In him there was no guile.

The first home for the aged of the archdiocese was established on the initiative of the clergymen's association of metropolitan New York; Archbishop Michael contributed not only his moral support but also financial assistance. His humanitarian concerns could fill a book, but the drives he inspired to help the victims of the earthquakes that almost destroyed the Ionian Islands in 1954 are especially memorable.

For more than two decades Holy Cross Greek Orthodox Theological School was no more than a priests' preparatory school. Those were difficult years, but Michael intended the school to become a center of theological activity as well. It was under his initiative that a dean with better academic credentials was appointed, several new and professionally trained faculty members were added, and a theological journal was established. The new dean was the Rev. Nicon Patrinakos, who held a doctorate from Oxford.

Michael was in favor of the Greek language in the liturgy; nevertheless it was during his primacy and through his own encouragement that the English sermon was introduced in Orthodox worship and Sunday School texts and instruction became bilingual.

Archbishop Michael had been involved in inter-Orthodox and interchurch relations from as early as 1927, when he represented the Ecumenical Patriarchate at the Faith and Order Conference held in Lausanne. He had participated in dialogues between Orthodox and Anglicans and among various Orthodox jurisdictions, and he encouraged both inter-Orthodox and interchurch relations. In the 1954 General Assembly of the World Council of Churches held in Evanston, Illinois, Archbishop Michael was elected one of the six presidents.

Perhaps one of the most controversial subjects during Michael's primacy was the effort of the archdiocese to impose upon all parishes the Uniform Parish Bylaws. Several congregations were disturbed because they viewed the archdiocese's plans as in violation of their own bylaws and as a further evidence of bureaucratic centralization. But all the archdiocese was trying to do was to eliminate chaos and introduce more harmony between the archdiocese and the parish. What Archbishop Athenagoras had tried to do through his personality and politics, Archbishop Michael tried to do through the adoption of a common constitution and common bylaws.

During the decade of the 1950s, not only the Greek but other ethnic Orthodox churches became better known. Several states granted offical recognition to Eastern Orthodoxy as a major faith, and for the first time the United States Congress adopted a bill that recognized the Eastern Orthodox in the Armed Forces as separate from Protestants and Catholics. The Orthodox in the Armed Forces were allowed to include "E.O." (Eastern Orthodox) on their tags. The fact that, for the first time in America's history, a Greek Orthodox archbishop was invited to offer prayers at the inauguration of President Dwight D. Eisenhower was an important event for the Orthodox, who had been overlooked for many decades.

But it was not only through the efforts of the archdiocese that more and more recognition of the Orthodox was achieved. Local initiative was just as important, if not more so. Several new church buildings, such as the Hagia Sophia in Los Angeles and the Annunciation Church of Milwaukee (designed by Frank Lloyd Wright) did a great deal to inform the public of Orthodoxy's presence in the United States. All in all, the decade of the 1950s was both innovative and extremely fruitful for the Church, which became the most important institution of the Greek American community at large.

The Church Marches Forward (1960–   )

The growth, spiritual awakening, and recognition of the Church's presence in America that began in the early 1950s increased in the early years of the 1960s. The leader in the new impetus was none other than the new archbishop, Iakovos.

Following the untimely death of Archbishop Michael in 1959, the Ecumenical Patriarchate elected the young and dynamic bishop of Melita, Iakovos Coucouzes, to become the new head of the American Church. He was enthroned in New York on April 1, 1959. The person, aspirations, and achievements of Archbishop Iakovos have been repeatedly described, and there is no need for a repetition here of well-known facts.

Every aspect of the Church's life and mission in the last twenty years has revealed movement forward. Archbishop Iakovos has been a dynamic, energetic, and progressive leader. The archdiocese's most successful efforts have been in the establishment of new congregations and the erection of innovatively designed Church buildings as well as religious education.

The decline of the American city and the emergence of suburbia, the soaring crime rate, the housing shortage, the spread of slums, racial tensions, and the prosperity of the Greek Orthodox contributed to their exodus to the suburbs. Many new and prosperous congregations came into being in the suburbs of cities such as New York, Philadelphia, Baltimore, Boston,

Detroit, and Chicago. The annual rate of community growth has been about 5 percent; there are no accurate statistics of membership growth.

The erection of new and architecturally innovative church buildings, such as the Annunciation Church in Milwaukee, Saint Nicholas Church in Flushing, New York, and the Ascension Church in Oakland, California, continued. While some congregations preferred to exist in their own cocoon, a few, especially those whose membership was composed overwhelmingly of third- and fourth-generation Greek Orthodox and many proselytes, became more cosmopolitan and socially involved. Nevertheless the Church as a whole continues to be an immigrant Church, concerned much more with itself and its own problems than with the outside world.

The archdiocese expanded both materially and organizationally. Several new departments were organized. The department of economic development and the department of religious education have indeed made many forward steps. The Philoptochos Society too has been reorganized along more professional lines.

Archbishop Iakovos has made tremendous efforts, providing leadership in resolving many internal and external issues, including racial conflict and inter-Orthodox and interchurch relations. He has issued a great number of substantive encyclicals and has delivered inspiring speeches. Nevertheless much remains to be achieved in several areas in the life of the church, such as liturgical renewal, social issues and family concerns, missionary work or involvement in society's problems, and issues facing clergymen either as celibates or as family men. There are scores of divorced clergymen and not a few, either married or celibate, who have left the Church, which does not provide professional counselling.

One healthy phenomenon in the Church's life of recent years is the emergence of criticism and the urge for internal dialogue, a result not only of the Logos movement but also of interest on the part of intellectuals and ordinary laymen. For example, there was a great deal of reaction against the archdiocese's pronouncements concerning the language problem, the development of the Church's institutions, such as Hellenic College, and the handling of the emergence of the Orthodox Church in America and of ecumenical relations.

But whatever the problems and the criticism, the institutional Church, whether as individual parish or as an archdiocese, moves on, and many of its faithful face the future with confidence. Indeed, when the conditions and problems of the Church of the first half of the twentieth century are compared with those of the third quarter, it must be admitted that much has been accomplished.

There are no accurate statistics concerning the number of members in the Greek Orthodox Church. My estimate is that there are no more than 2,000,000. The number of Greek Orthodox families that support the archdiocese through the annual contribution (now the *eikosidollarion,* or $20 annual obligation) is a little over 100,000, while at the end of 1973 there were 91,413 Greek Orthodox families that supported local churches by paying an average annual contribution or dues of $74.00 (excluding Sunday offerings). Thus the Greek Orthodox faithful who are supporting "members" of a local church should be placed at about 500,000. Those who do not "belong" cannot be more than 1,500,000.

The chancellor's report to the twenty-second Biennial Clergy-Laity Congress provides the following information: In June 1974, there were 473 houses of worship served by 604 priests. The educational background of the clergy has greatly improved: of the 604 priests, 372 possess bachelor's degrees in theology; 147 have earned master's degrees in theology, in philosophy, history, economics, psychology, or in some other field; 21 have earned doctorates in theology or philosophy; and the remaining 64 are graduates of preparatory seminaries or priests' training schools. The archbishop, as primate of the archdiocese, heads a synod of twelve bishops (including one for Canada, one for Central America, and one for South America).

In addition to Hellenic College, which now incorporates both Holy Cross Greek Orthodox Theological School and Saint Basil's Teachers College, the archdiocese has under its aegis 22 fully accredited parochial schools, serving over 6,500 students; and 401 "afternoon" community schools of Greek language and culture, with some 28,000 students and 760 teachers. Each church has one or two Sunday schools, and there are 596 catechetical schools, serving close to 65,000 students.

In the area of philanthropic institutions and social welfare, the archdiocese could have done much better. There are only a few homes for the aged, orphanages, and reformatory institutions, all of which were established as a result of private initiative rather than under the archdiocese's direction. But there are 438 chapters of the Philoptochos Society that look after the needy. The work of the society is very commendable indeed, but this is not the place to write more about it.

While in the early 1960s there was a deep concern for public recognition of the Greek Orthodox Church and Orthodoxy in general, recent clergy-laity congresses have emphasized the need for a reorientation, for a self-examination self-study. This, of course, is a more serious approach, which in the long run will gain for the Church more respect and recognition than other measures.

In the last twenty years commendable progress has been made in the areas of inter-Orthodox and interchurch relations. The Orthodox in America have been one in doctrine, worship, and ethos, but socially not so close. With the exception of the late nineteenth century and the early 1900s, when there were pan-Orthodox churches and closer ties, the relations among Orthodox jurisdictions were indifferent, if not cold, for a few decades. In order to achieve closer cooperation, in 1960 the Standing Conference of Canonical Orthodox Bishops in the Americas was established

> to serve as an agency to centralize and coordinate the mission of the Church. It acts as a clearing house to focus the efforts of the church on common concerns and to avoid duplication and overlapping of services and agencies. Special departments are devoted to campus work, Christian education, military and other chaplaincies, regional clergy fellowships and ecumenical relations.

To be sure, goodwill has been fostered, but SCOBA is expected to foster better relations among all Orthodox. Few of the rank and file of Orthodox Christians know of SCOBA's existence, and not much has been done to bring either the people or the clergy into closer cooperation.

In addition to inter-Orthodox relations, the archdiocese has been active in ecumenical relations. In 1962 the Anglican-Orthodox Theological Consultation was organized to promote better relations between the Orthodox and Episcopalians. There are also the Orthodox-Catholic and the Orthodox-Reformed Theological Consultations. The activities of all three are limited to annual meetings and to the exchange of papers and opinions on various theological issues. It is too early to assess the influence of these commissions on the theological minds of the parties concerned. Nevertheless, they have been interesting theological forums.

Epilogue

There have been stages in the development of the Greek Orthodox Church in America, each with its strengths and its weaknesses. Whatever the future historical evaluation may be, the fact is that the Greek Orthodox have walked a hard road. In 1972 they observed the fiftieth anniversary of their archdiocese. Notwithstanding their individualism and national pride, they have now moved a little outside their own circle and have made significant contributions to American society.

There are numerous American citizens who are members of the Greek Orthodox Church and occupy influential positions in American life, in politics, in the hard sciences, in the arts, in business, in music, in athletics, and in other areas of endeavor.

Considering their proportion to the total population, one may assert that Greek Americans have been greatly involved in the political, economic, educational, and social life of the nation. The following information will illustrate these remarks. At the present time there are several Greek Americans in the United States Congress—two Senators (Paul Sarbanes of Maryland and Paul Tsongas of Massachusetts) and four members in the House of Representatives (Gus Yatron of Pennsylvania; Olympia Bouchles Snowe of Maine, the youngest woman ever elected in the United States Congress; Nick Mavroules of Massachusetts; and L. A. Bafalis of Florida). Others who in recent years have served in the Federal Government include Vice-President Spiro T. Agnew and Congressmen John Brademas of Indiana, Nick Galigianakis of North Carolina, and Peter Kyros of Maine. It is not irrelevant to mention that a few years ago the state of Massachusetts simultaneously had a governor (Michael Dukakis), a senator (Tsongas) and a congressman (Mavroules) of the Greek Orthodox tradition. There are many Greek Americans who have served or currently serve as representatives in state assemblies and in city governments—such as George Christopher, former mayor of San Francisco; Lee Alexander, mayor of Syracuse, New York; George Athanson, mayor of Hartford, Connecticut; John Roussakis, mayor of Savannah, Georgia; Helen Boosalis, mayor of Lincoln, Nebraska, and president of the United States Conference of Mayors. Several more have occupied high positions in several departments of the federal government, such as Peter G. Peterson, former secretary of commerce; John N. Nassikas, chairman of the National Power Commission; Eugene T. Rossides, former assistant secretary of the treasury; Andrew E. Manatos, former assistant secretary of commerce; Thomas Karamachinas, chief of operations, CIA; Achilles N. Sakellarides, inspector of economic and military assistance programs for the State Department.

In the arts, literature, and communications there are such internationally known artists as Dimitri Mitropoulos and Maria Callas, and several more who have distinguished themselves: Elia Kazan, the film director; Alexander Scourby, stage actor; Andrew Sarris, film critic; Theodore Kalem, drama critic; Ike Pappas, a leading reporter of CBS; Harry Mark Petrakis, the son of a priest and the author of several acclaimed novels; George Maharis, George Chakiris, Telly Savalas, actors; John Cassavetes, actor and film director, and James Galanos, the fashion designer.

During the last twenty years several Greek Americans have become prominent in national sports, especially in baseball, football, and basketball; among them are Harry Agganis, Gus Niarchos, Gus Triandos, Alex Grammas, Milt Pappas, Lou Tsioropoulos, and Alex Karras. Many Greeks have been involved in commerce and trade, and several Greek Americans occupy high positions in the hierarchy of American corporations, among them William Tavoulareas, president of Mobil; John Philips, president of Raytheon; Anthony Thomopoulos, president of ABC, Entertainment Division; George Hatzopoulos, president of Thermo-Electron Corporation; Andrew Kariotis, president of Alpha Industries; K. Pontikes, chairman of Combis Co.; George Soros, described by the *Institutional Investor* magazine as the world's greatest money manager, to mention only some.

Perhaps in no other field have Greek Americans contributed more than in education—primary, secondary, and higher—either as administrators (such as Matina Souretis Horner, president of Radcliffe College; John Brademas, president of New York University; Peter Diamantopoulos, President of Sonoma State University in California; Peter Liacouras, dean of Temple University School of Law) or as instructors. There are several thousand professors on the faculties of American and Canadian universities. Suffice it to mention here that there are some thirty-five professors, from the rank of assistant to full professor, on the faculty of the renowned Massachusetts Institute of Technology.

Elementary and high school educators are estimated at many thousands. There is no major community without Greek Orthodox physicians, lawyers, pharmacists, chemists, engineers, and other scientists. Several of these professionals are internationally famous. True, some are indifferent to Church activities, but most have benefitted from the Church and remain faithful, if not to the creed at least to its culture. Indeed, as *The New York Times* in a recent editorial commended, the "two million Americans of Greek descent" have been "influential and articulate" in matters affecting the affairs of the nation.

Without doubt, the Greek Orthodox community is a creative, albeit sometimes highly individualistic and distinctive, entity in American life. Yet is is also mindful of its Christian Orthodox commitment and its Greek heritage. In fact, the weight of this double tradition is the source of the Greek Orthodox Church's anxieties and problems. Often there is a conflict between faith and culture, which is not easy to resolve. Because of this double heritage one congregation may emphasize religious commitment while another may stress cultural and social values. To be sure, for several years it was the common Greek heritage that gave coherence and identity to the Orthodox of Greek origins, and sociological reasons may have contributed more to the organization of the Church than religious ones, but in the last twenty-five years the religious factor has been given prominence. A few Greek Orthodox communities that are more social organizations than religious institutions may still exist, but on a whole the spiritual and religious progress in many communities is very evident.

Of course, the question has been raised whether Greek Orthodoxy can survive in its present doctrinal, ethical, and liturgical forms. History indicates that creeds and ideas that are not consistent with the everyday experience of the people or that lack strong commitment cannot long survive. This means that no matter what theologians and churchmen propose, the acceptance of a theology or a religious system depends on the people who experience a life that fits that theology or religious truth. There is a need for self-study and self-evaluation. Whether the Greek Orthodox in America will be able to preserve and perpetuate their Christian doctrines and beliefs and whether they will be able to sustain themselves under the weight of their cultural tradition are major problems, which should preoccupy the mind and work of the Church's lay and clerical leadership.

In the past the Greek Orthodox of America have proved tenacious, diligent, energetic, patient, and idealistic. It is hoped that their children and their children's children will follow in their footsteps.

Selected Bibliography

The author is indebted to the following sources and secondary works.

On Religion as a Preparation for Christianity

BERGSON, HENRI. *The Two Sources of Morality and Religion.* Translated by R. Ashley Audra and others. New York: 1954.

CAPPS, WALTER H., ed. *Ways of Understanding Religion.* New York: 1972.

DAWSON, CHRISTOPHER H. *Religion and Culture.* New York: 1958.

JAMES, WILLIAM. *The Varieties of Religious Experience.* New York: 1929.

JURGI, EDWARD J. *The Christian Interpretation of Religion.* New York: 1952.

LECOMTE DU NOÜY, PIERRE. *Human Destiny.* New York, London, Toronto: 1948.

MAVRODES, GEORGE. *Belief in God.* New York: 1970.

MENZIES, ALLAN. *History of Religion.* New York: 1917.

O'DEA, THOMAS F. *The Sociology of Religion.* Englewood Cliffs, N.J.: 1966.

OTTO, RUDOLF. *The Ideal of the Holy.* Tranlated by John W. Harvey. New York: 1958.

RADIN, PAUL. *Monotheism Among Primitive Peoples.* London: 1924.

RANDALL, JOHN H., JR. *The Meaning of Religion for Man.* New York: 1968.

SCHMIDT, WILHELM. *The Origin and Growth of Religion.* Translated by H. J. Rose. London: 1931.

———. *Primitive Revelation.* St. Louis, Mo.: 1939.

TAYLOR, A. E. *Does God Exist?* New York: 1947.

On Later Judaism, Greek Thought, and Early Christianity

ANGUS, S. *The Religious Quests of the Graeco-Roman World.* 1929. Reprint New York: 1967.

BYRON, ROBERT. *The Byzantine Achievement.* 1929. Reprint New York: 1964.

CHADWICK, HENRY. *Early Christian Thought and the Classical Tradition.* New York: 1966.

DODD, C. H. *The Bible and the Greeks.* Part I. London: 1935.

DODDS, E. R. *The Greeks and the Irrational.* Berkeley, Calif.: 1971.

EVERY, GEORGE. *The Byzantine Patriarchate.* London: 1962.

FLOROVSKY, GEORGES. "Patristics and Modern Theology." In *Procès-verbaux du Premier Congrès de Théologie Orthodoxe,* edited by H. S. Alivisatos, pp. 238–242. Athens: 1939.

GLOVER, TERROT REAVELEY. *The Conflict of Religions in the Early Roman Empire.* Boston: 1960.

GRANT, FREDERICK C. *Hellenistic Religions. The Age of Syncretism.* New York: 1953.

GRANT, FREDERICK C. *Roman Hellenism and the New Testament.* New York: 1962.

HADAS, MOSES. *Hellenistic Culture.* New York: 1959.

HATCH, EDWIN. *The Influence of Greek Ideas on Christianity.* New York: 1957.

HENGEL, MARTIN. *Judaism and Hellenism.* Translated by John Bowden. 2 vols. Philadelphia: 1974.

———. *Jews, Greeks and Barbarians.* Translated by John Bowden. Philadelphia: 1980.

JAEGER, WERNER. *Early Christianity and Greek Paideia.* Cambridge, Mass.: 1961.

———. *The Theology of the Early Greek Philsophers.* Oxford: 1947.

LIEBERMANN, SAUL. *Greek in Jewish Palestine.* New York: 1942.

———. *Hellenism in Jewish Palestine.* New York: 1950.

NILSSON, MARTIN P. *A History of Greek Religion.* second edition. New York: 1964.

———. *Greek Piety.* Translated by Herbert Jennings Rose. New York: 1969.

NOCK. A. D. *Early Gentile Christianity and Its Hellenistic Background.* New York: 1964.

———. *Conversion: The Old and the New in Religion from Alexander the Great to Augustine of Hippo.* Oxford: 1933.

PETERS, F. E. *The Harvest of Hellenism.* New York: 1970.

RAHNER, HUGO. *Greek Myths and Christian Mystery.* Translated by Brian Battershaw. New York: 1963.

RANDALL, JOHN HERMAN. *Hellenistic Ways of Deliverance and the Making of the Christian Synthesis.* New York: 1970.

SCHWABE, M. and LIFSHITZ, B. *Beth She'arim. Vol. II The Greek Inscriptions.* New Brunswick, N.J.: 1974.

SHIEL, JAMES. *Greek Thought and the Rise of Christianity.* New York: 1968.
TCHERIKOVER, VICTOR. *Hellenistic Civilization and the Jews.* Translated by S. Applebaum. New York: 1977.
ZIELINSKI, THADDEUS. *The Religion of Ancient Greece.* Translated by George Rapall Noyes. Oxford: 1926.

On Orthodox Faith, History, and Practice

Sources

The Bible, Revised Standard Version
Apostolike Diakonia tes Ekklesias tes Hellados. *Bibliotheke Hellenon Pateron kai Ekklesiastikon Syggrafeon.* Athens: 1955–.
BARCLAY, WILLIAM. *Commentaries to the Books of the New Testament.* Daily Study Bible Series. 15 vols. Philadelphia: 1956–1960.
KARMIRIS, IOANNIS. *Dogmatica et symbolica monumenta Orthodoxae Catholicae Ecclesiae.* 2nd ed. Vol. 1. Athens: 1960. Vol. 2, Graz: 1968.
A Select Library of the Nicene and Post-Nicene Fathers. First and Second Series. 28 vols. Grand Rapids, Mich.: 1956.
TREMBELAS, PANAGIOTIS N., *Commentaries to the New Testament.* 7 vols. Athens: 1937–1955. Several patristic passages have been compiled from Trembelas's commentaries.
The Writings of the Ante-Nicene Fathers. 10 vols. Grand Rapids, Mich.: 1956.

Modern Works

ALIVIZATOS, HAMILCAR S. *E Hellenike Orthodoxos Ekklesia.* Athens: 1955.
AMERICAN SCIENTIFIC AFFILIATION. *Modern Science and Christian Faith.* Second Edition. Wheaton, Ill.: 1950.
ANDROUTSOS, CHRISTOS. *Dogmatike tes Orthodoxou Anatolikes Ekklesias.* 2d. ed. Athens: 1956.
BASILEIADIS, NIKOLAOS P. *E Christianike Pistis eis ton Aiona tes Epistemes.* Athens: 1975.
BIOT, RENÉ. *What is Life.* New York: 1959.
BRATSIOTIS, PANAYOTIS *Fundamental Principles and Chief Characteristics of the Orthodox Church* in *The Orthodox Ethos*, ed. A. J. Philippou. Oxford, 1964. pp. 23–31.
————, ed. *Die Orthodoxe Kirche in griechischer Sicht.* 2 vols. Stuttgart: 1959–1960.
BULGAKOV, SERGIUS. *The Orthodox Church.* Translated by Elizabeth S. Gram. London: 1936.

CALLINICOS, CONSTANTINE. *Ta Themelia tes Pisteos.* 2nd ed. Athens: 1958. English translation by G. Dimopoulos. Scranton, PA: 1975.

———. *O Christianikos Naos kai ta Teloumena en Auto.* 2nd ed. Athens: 1958.

Christian Union of Scientists, eds. *Tria Dokimia peri Orthodoxos.* Athens: 1962.

CONSTANTELOS, DEMETRIOS J. *Byzantine Philanthropy and Social Welfare.* Parts 1 and 2. Rutgers Byzantine Series, No. 4. New Brunswick, N.J.: 1968.

———. "The Lover of Mankind," *The Way,* Vol. 9, No. 2: pp. 98–106.

———. "The Evangelical Character of the Orthodox Church." *Journal of Ecumenical Studies,* Vol. 9, No. 3.

DVORNIK, FRANCIS. *The Photian Schism.* Cambridge: 1948.

———. *Byzantine Missions Among the Slavs.* New Brunswick, N.J.: 1970.

EVDOKIMOV, P. *L'Orthodoxie.* Paris: 1959.

FLOROVSKY, GEORGES. *Bible, Church, Tradition: An Eastern Orthodox View.* Belmont, Mass.: 1972.

GAVIN, FRANK. *Some Aspects of Contemporary Greek Orthodox Thought.* Milwaukee: 1936.

KARMIRES, IOANNIS. *A Synopsis of the Dogmatic Theology of the Orthodox Catholic Church.* Athens: 1957. English translation by G. Dimopoulos. Scranton, PA: 1973.

KOKKINAKIS, ATHENAGORAS. *Parents and Priests as Servants of Redemption.* New York: 1958.

LOSSKY, VLADIMIR. *The Mystical Theology of the Eastern Church.* London: 1957.

MATHER, KIRTLEY F. *Science in Search of God.* New York: 1928.

MEYENDORFF, J.; AFANASSIEFF, N.; SCHMEMANN, A.; AND KOULOMZINE, N. *The Primacy of Peter in the Orthodox Church.* London: 1963.

MEYENDORFF, JEAN. *The Orthodox Church.* New York: 1962.

A MONK OF THE EASTERN CHURCH. *Orthodox Spirituality.* London: 1957.

PAPADOPOULOS, CHRYSOSTOM. *H Orthodox Anatolike Ekklesia.* Athens: 1954.

———. *E Ekklesia tes Hellados.* 2nd ed. Athens: 1951.

PLOUMIDES, E. *Eisagoge ston Christianismon.* Athens: 1959.

POLLARD, WILLIAM G. *Chance and Providence.* New York: 1958.

RAMM, BERNARD. *The Christian View of Science and Scripture.* Grand Rapids, Mich.: 1956.

RICAUT, PAUL. *The Present State of the Greek and Armenian Churches Anno Christi 1678.* London: 1679; New York: 1970.

RICHARDSON, ALAN. *Christian Apologetics.* New York: 1947.

RUNCIMAN, STEVEN. *The Eastern Schism.* Oxford: 1955.

———. *The Great Church in Captivity.* Cambridge: 1968.

SCHMEMANN, ALEXANDER. *For the Life of the World.* New York: 1963.
———. *The Historical Road of Eastern Orthodoxy.* New York: 1963.
SMETHURST, ARTHUR F. *Modern Science and Christian Beliefs.* New York: 1955.
THEODOROU, ANDREAS. *E Ousia tes Orthodoxias.* Athens: 1961.

TREMBELAS, PANAGIOTIS N. *Apologetikai Meletai,* 3 vols., Athens: 1965–1971.
———. *Dogmatike tes Orthodoxou Katholikes Ekklesias,* 3 vols. Athens: 1959–1961.
WARE, TIMOTHY. *The Orthodox Church.* Baltimore: 1963.
ZANKOV, STEFAN. *The Eastern Orthodox Church.* Translated and edited by D. A. Lowrie. Milwaukee, Wisc.: 1929.
ZERNOV, NICOLAS. *Eastern Christendom.* New York: 1961.
Zoe, Brotherhood of Theologians. *E. Episteme Omilei.* Athens: 1949.
———, eds. *Thelogia, Aletheia kai Zoe.* Athens: 1962.

On the Greek Orthodox in America

AHLSTROM, SYDNEY E. *A Religious History of the American People,* pp. 985–994. New Haven, Conn.: 1972.
BURGESS, THOMAS. *Greeks in America.* Boston: 1913.
———. *Foreign-born Americans and Their Children.* New York: 1921.
CONSTANTELOS, DEMETRIOS J. "Ena Gramma tou proen Athenon Meletiou pros ton Hypourgon ton Exoterikon Charles Evans Hughes." *Ekklesia,* Vol. 50, No. 1 (1–15 May, 1973): pp. 250–252.
———, ed. *Encyclicals and Documents of the Greek Orthodox Archdiocese.* New York: 1974.
———. "Oi Protoi Hellenes tes Amerikes tou 1768." *Aktines,* Vol. 27 (Dec. 1964): pp. 377–380. Translated into English by Dr. Leonidas Petrakis and printed in *Hellenic Review,* Vol. VI, No. 11 (Sept. 1965): pp. 18–19.
DOUMOURAS, ALEXANDER. "Greek Orthodox Communities in America Before World War I." *St. Vladimir's Seminary Quarterly,* Vol. 11, No. 4 (1967): pp. 172–192.
EMHARDT, WILLIAM CHAUNCEY, and others. *The Eastern Church in the Western World.* Milwaukee, Wisc.: 1928. Reprint, New York: 1970.
GRIGORIEFF, DIMITRY. "Historical Background of Orthodoxy in America." *St. Vladimir's Seminary Quarterly,* Vol. 5, No. 1–2 (1961): pp. 3–53.
IAKOVOS (ARCHBISHOP OF NORTH AND SOUTH AMERICA). "The Fifty Years of Life and Development of the Greek Orthodox Archdiocese of the Americas, 1922–1971." *Yearbook 1972.* Greek Orthodox

Archdiocese of North and South America, pp. 10–13. New York: 1972.

KONTARGYRES, THEODORE N. *O Apodemos Hellenismos tes Amerikes.* 2nd ed. Athens: 1964.

KOURIDES, PETER T. *The Evolution of the Greek Orthodox Church in America and Its Present Problems.* New York: 1959.

LACEY, THOMAS J. *Our Greek Immigrants.* New York: 1918.

MALAFOURIS, BABES. *Hellenes tes Amerikes 1528–1948.* New York: 1948.

MOSCHOS, CHARLES C., JR. *Greek Americans.* Englewood Cliffs, N.J.: 1980.

Nea Estia. Vol. 58 (1955) several articles.

PANAGOPOULOS, E. *New Smyrna: An Eighteenth Century Greek Odyssey.* Gainesville, Fla.: 1966.

PAPAIOANNOU, GEORGE. *From Mars Hill to Manhattan.* Minneapolis, Minn.: 1976.

ROSEN, BERNARD. "Race, Ethnicity, and the Achievement Syndrome." *American Sociological Review,* Vol. 24 (1959): pp. 47–60.

SALOUTOS, THEODORE. "The Greek Orthodox Church in the United States and Assimilation." *International Migration Review,* Vol. VII, No. 4 (Winter 1973): pp. 395–407.

———. *The Greeks in the United States.* Cambridge, Mass., 1964.

———. "Stirrings in the New World." *Greek Orthodox Congress XXII,* pp. 46–50. Greek Orthodox Archdiocese, New York: 1974.

SCOURBY, ALICE. *Third Generation Greek Americans: A Study of Religious Attitudes.* Ph.D. thesis, New School for Social Research, New York, 1967.

STYLIANOPOULOS, THEODORE. "The Orthodox Church in America." *The Annals of the American Academy of Political and Social Science,* Vol. 387. (1970): pp. 41–48.

TSOUMAS, GEORGE J. "The Founding Years of Holy Cross Greek Orthodox Theological School." *The Greek Orthodox Theological Review,* Vol. XII, No. 3 (1967): pp. 241–282.

TRUEDLY, MARY B. "Formal Organization and the Americanization Process with Special Reference to the Greeks in Boston." *American Sociological Review,* Vol. XIV (Feb. 1949): pp. 44–55.

VOLAITES, CONSTANTINE. "The Orthodox Church in the United States as Viewed from the Social Sciences." *St. Vladimir's Seminary Quarterly,* Vol. 5, No. 1–2 (1961): pp. 63–87.

XENIDES, J. P. *The Greeks in America.* New York: 1922.

ZIOGAS, ELIAS K. *O Hellenismos tes Amerikes Autos o Agnostos.* Athens: 1958.

ZOTOS, STEPHANOS. *Hellenic Presence in America.* Wheaton, Ill.: 1976.

ZOUSTIS, VASILEIOS TH. *O en Amerike Hellenismos kai e Drasis Autou.* New York: 1954.

Index
of Biblical Quotations

Index
of Proper Names & Subjects